BULLYING
HURTS

TEACHING KINDNESS THROUGH

READ ALOUDS AND

GUIDED CONVERSATIONS

Lester L. Laminack and **Reba M. Wadsworth**

HEINEMANN
Portsmouth, NH

Heinemann
361 Hanover Street
Portsmouth, NH 03801–3912
www.heinemann.com

Offices and agents throughout the world

The authors and publisher wish to thank those who have generously given permission to reprint borrowed material:

Excerpts from the *Olweus Bullying Prevention Program* © Hazelden Foundation, 2012. Used with permission from violencepreventionworks.org.

Excerpts from the *Bully Free Program* by Allan L. Beane, Ph.D. Copyright © 2012 Bully Free Systems, LLC, www.bullyfree.com. Used by permission of the author.

Excerpts from the *Common Core State Standards* © Copyright 2010. National Governors Association Center for Best Practices and Council of Chief State School Officers. All rights reserved.

"Sample Antibullying Pledge" adapted from *The Everything Parent's Guide to Dealing with Bullies* by Deborah Carpenter with Christopher J. Ferguson. Copyright © 2009 by F&W Media, Inc. Published by Adams Media, an F&W Media, Inc. company. Used by permission of the publisher.

"Hello Neighbor" song movements from *Responsive Classroom Level I Resource Book.* Turners Falls, MA: Northeast Foundation for Children. Copyright © 2007. Used by permission of the publisher.

Library of Congress Cataloging-in-Publication Data
Laminack, Lester L.
   Bullying hurts : teaching kindness through read alouds and guided conversations / Lester L. Laminack and Reba M. Wadsworth.
        p. cm.
   Includes bibliographical references.
   ISBN-13: 978-0-325-04356-2
   ISBN-10: 0-325-04356-6
   1. Bullying in schools—United States—Prevention. 2. Bullying in schools—United States—Psychological aspects. I. Wadsworth, Reba M. II. Title.
   LB3013.32.L36 2012
   371.5'8—dc23   2012007927

Editor: Holly Kim Price
Production: Victoria Merecki
Cover design: Matthew Simmons
Interior design: Monica Ann Crigler
Typesetting: Eric Rosenbloom, Kirby Mountain Composition
Manufacturing: Steve Bernier

Printed in the United States of America on acid-free paper
16 15 14 13   ML   2 3 4 5

Dedication

For the victims of bullying behaviors, may you know your worth as a member of the human family, embrace your humanity, and see the good present in the world around you. May kindness heal your hurt.

For the bystanders who witness, may you find your voice, feel your worth, recognize the inherent worth of others, and find the strength to stand up for those in need of your support. May kindness encourage and embolden you.

For those who resist the bullying behaviors of others or defend the victims of that behavior, may you know the value of your strength and caring. May kindness continue to give you clarity to recognize the opportunity to support those in need.

For those who have, for whatever reason, come to believe that bullying behavior increases your dignity and worth, may you find value in your own humanity and come to recognize that all that makes you human is also present in every other person. May you find your identity in your strengths and talents, your power in the ability to control yourself and not in the control of others, and respect for yourself that will enable you to respect the humanity common among all people. May kindness be the light that shines in your darkest moments.

CONTENTS

ACKNOWLEDGMENTS

The topic is a serious one. There are young people taking their own lives. Others are living with wounds and scars. Some may carry the burden for a lifetime. Bullying is a serious topic, and we do not take the responsibility of this project lightly. *Bullying Hurts* has been a work of passion and commitment evolving from years of living, teaching, thinking, and work.

We are grateful to the many people who have contributed to the conversations that shaped our thinking, to those who have suggested books, articles, and Web sites as resources. We are grateful to those who shared titles of picture books and novels to explore and to those who shared personal accounts, classroom stories, and words of encouragement as to the need for a project such as this one.

We are grateful to those teachers who opened their hearts and minds to new ways of thinking and opened their doors and schedules to allow us an opportunity to step inside their teaching and try our ideas on for fit. These teachers, from the Decatur school system in Decatur, Alabama, include Kristi Adams, Melissa Dickman, Janet Foster, Mary Kay Hodges, Christy Wadsworth, and Maria Garrison. And in Asheville, North Carolina, at the Francine Delaney New School for Children, our gratitude is owed to Rosyln Clapp, Naomi Marotta, Melissa Murphy, and Jessica Roberts.

We are grateful to Kate Montgomery whose immediate support for this idea never wavered. Your kind heart and generous spirit nurtured both the writing and the writers.

We are grateful to Holly Kim Price whose keen eye and insights helped us tighten the focus and bring greater clarity to each page. You made this process a joy.

And finally we are grateful to Lesa Scott who continues to believe in the power of teachers and their right to have access to the best. You create conditions that encourage us to create, to stretch, and to risk in that endeavor.

INTRODUCTION

There has been tremendous attention given to bullying recently. National news coverage, documentaries and special reports, magazine and newspaper articles, and campaigns featuring high-profile individuals have been dedicated to confronting this plague. All this heightened awareness has brought much needed attention to an age-old problem. And this spotlight has helped us understand the scale of the issue.

Now let's zoom in and get a close-up view. Let's try to understand through an adult lens what life is like inside the mind and body of the bullied victim. Try to imagine the difficulty of shutting off your fear in order to find sleep. Try to imagine the anxiety of waking only to realize today is a school day and you can't escape. Try to imagine spending your day on guard, knowing it will happen, just not knowing when or where. We want to help you imagine what it may be like to be one of the 160,000 children in the United States who skip school daily out of fear of being bullied. Imagine that you experience the same sort of taunting, teasing, verbal, emotional, and physical bullying in your adult life.

Take a moment and just imagine . . .

Each morning as you come into work you find your personal things are in disarray. Each day there is something more. The first morning someone has drawn horns with permanent marker on the photo of you and a loved one. The next morning all your pens are gone and pencils are broken. If you leave for a break, you return to find files deleted from your computer screen. Each day there is something new, you never know what or when it will happen, but you are always tense just knowing it is going to happen again. Each day you go to work anxious, no one, not even your friends, step up to help. When you voice concern everyone says it's just a prank, someone is just having fun. Your supervisor tells you to grow up and get your work done.

Imagine . . .

At work you have a tight circle of friends who always gather in the break room for lunch. Lately a couple of them are pulling away from the others. They eat alone and rarely join in the group conversation anymore. Then one day as you enter the break room you notice everyone is sitting together again. You smile and step toward the table to join them. Everyone stops talking and looks in the direction of those two who have rejoined the group. They give the group a look and everyone sits in silence when you join. No one looks at you. No one speaks to you. The next day as you enter, the room falls silent and you notice a chair missing from the table. There is no space for you to join. Everyone looks at his or her food and no one will make eye contact with you. The two begin to whisper with others and all of them chuckle while looking in your direction. This isolation escalates and begins to ooze out into the workspace until you have no one who will even look at you.

Imagine . . .

You are standing in line at a fast-food restaurant. You are rushed and eager to get back to work on time. You are reading the menu, trying to decide what you will order, when out of nowhere you feel a stinging pain, your head jerks violently to the left, sunglasses fly off your face, and pain throbs in the back of your head. The voice behind you booms, "Get out of the way, moron, it's the same damn menu they've had for twenty years. You ought to know what you want before you get in line. Move! I don't have all day." You bend down to retrieve your glasses, tears stream down your face. As you look up a few people are staring at you but say nothing, most people are looking away and no one is saying anything to the guy who whacked you and stepped ahead in line. No one comes to your aid. No one.

Imagine these are not isolated occurrences; rather they become a routine that you simply must adjust to. Imagine how your evenings would be spent worrying over getting through the next day. Imagine feeling so defenseless, so alone, so anxious and fearful. Imagine you actually come to believe that no one sees you as worthy of his or her assistance, or attention, or care. To others you are less than human. Just imagine . . .

How long could you endure?

As adults we know scenarios such as these are very unlikely to happen to us. However, there are students who can report similar scenarios happening every day in school hallways, stairways, cafeterias, playgrounds, gymnasiums, on buses and in classrooms everywhere. Wherever there are groups of children, bullying is likely to take place sooner or later.

Bullying, like bad weather, respects no boundaries. Bullying moves in on victims without regard for geography, socioeconomic status, race, ethnicity, religion, politics, age, gender, or sexual orientation. It is true that some groups are more likely to become a target than others. It is true that boys are more likely to participate in physical bullying and girls are more likely to engage in social and emotional bullying. However, one Google search or one visit to YouTube will prove there are exceptions to every pattern you can identify among the behaviors of students who bully.

Bullying isn't a new phenomenon. In recent years, however, the world has witnessed an increase in the frequency and intensity of bullying in our schools. The increased incidence of bullying in all its forms (physical aggression, verbal abuse, emotional bullying, and cyberbullying) has resulted in psychological and physical harm to the victims and, in too many instances, the suicides of children and youth. Bullying, now in the spotlight, is receiving long overdue media attention. Perhaps this will help raise the public awareness necessary to bring this behavior to an end.

School leadership, classroom teachers, staff developers, and parents are searching for support. Adults in the lives of young people are searching for help, for what to do, and for how to intervene. There is general agreement in the professional community that a proactive stance is necessary. Waiting until an act of bullying has occurred is shortsighted, if not dangerous.

We are writing this book, *Bullying Hurts: Teaching Kindness Through Read Alouds and Guided Conversations*, in hopes that it will provide you with new insights and language that can help you lead your students toward kindness, civility, and human compassion as a way of being.

Data on bullying in the United States has been included to highlight the need to address the issue full on from the first day of kindergarten through the day of graduation from twelfth grade. There is information to assist you in identifying the various forms of bullying behaviors and to understand how and why the behaviors may arise. In addition, there is information to help identify children who may be either a bully or a victim of bullying.

We have deliberately connected this work to the anchor standards for reading in the Common Core College and Career Readiness Standards document to demonstrate how teachers can legitimately engage students in the work as a part of the curriculum. We offer a format for focused read aloud experiences using thoughtfully selected picture books through a series of five layers of developing insight and empathy. Each of the five layers is presented in sequence and includes a set of essential understandings to be developed through the experiences and conversations within the layer. We present a guide for each of the five featured books within each layer and recommend a framework for moving through each book. There are also suggestions for building community and extending the thinking between focused read aloud experiences. Following the five layers of focused read aloud experiences and guided conversations, we include an extensive list of other picture books that may be used. We clustered them under the five layers for ease of use and as alternatives to the titles featured in each of the five layers. We also include appendices with a sample letter you may wish to send to parents/caregivers as you begin the project, a sample antibully-ing contract, a list of community-building activities, a list of additional resources, and a bibliography.

Bullying Hurts: Teaching Kindness Through Read Alouds and Guided Conversations is written to assist you in leading your children to the threshold of their own under-standing about the need for kindness and compassion, about the responsibility to self and others as members of the human family, and about developing an under-standing of what bullying is and why it happens. We believe these insights can move us forward in bringing kindness, civility, and human compassion into the culture of school.

We believe focused read aloud experiences with carefully selected children's liter-ature followed by guided conversations is one way you can create a climate in your classroom, school, or district where bullying is not an accepted or rewarded behavior. A climate where an individual's humanity and human dignity trump any difference(s) and kindness is the order of the day. A climate where students, all students, feel both physically and emotionally safe. A climate where students thrive physically, emotion-ally, and academically.

We hear a lot about bullying on the news and in conversations with colleagues and parents. So let's be clear about what we mean by the word *bullying*. The American Psychological Association (2012) defines *bullying* as "a form of aggressive behavior in which someone intentionally and repeatedly causes another person injury or discom-fort. Bullying can take the form of physical contact, words or more subtle actions. . . . The bullied individual typically has trouble defending him or herself and does nothing to 'cause' the bullying." Beane (2009) adds that in any bullying situation, there is an imbalance of power.

What's at the core of this behavior?

Barbara Coloroso (2011) asserts that bullying is not about anger. Rather, it arises from feeling superior and seeing no value in selected others. "It is about contempt—a powerful feeling of dislike toward someone considered to be worthless, inferior or un-deserving of respect. Bullying is arrogance in action. Once kids believe that someone is 'less than them' they can harm that child without feeling any empathy, compassion or shame" (52).

Swearer, Espelage, and Napolitano (2009) report that "bullies can be socially skilled, have normal to heightened theory of mind, are in some cases viewed as popular in friendship groups, and are sought after as students begin dating relationships" (35).

Information about bullying suggests that there are three interrelated reasons why students bully (Olweus Bullying Prevention Program 2011):

1. Students who bully have strong needs for power and (negative) dominance.
2. Students who bully find satisfaction in causing injury and suffering to other students.
3. Students who bully are often rewarded in some way for their behavior with material or psychological rewards.

In kid-friendly terms, we might say,

> The reason why one kid would want to bully another kid is this: when you make someone feel bad, you gain power over him or her. Power makes people feel like they're better than another person, and then that makes them feel really good about themselves. Power also makes you stand out from the crowd. It's a way to get attention from other kids, and even from adults. (PBS Kids 2009)

This information further suggests that the behavior of bystanders can actually build up the status of a bully. When a bully has an audience that doesn't intervene, the bully gains power both in the group and in his or her own self-image.

How are acts of bullying manifested?

It's My Life, a website for kids funded by the Corporation for Public Broadcasting and produced by Castle Works Productions, offers a very kid-friendly explanation of three forms of bullying: physical, verbal, and relationship. Additional information to support educators and parents can be found from Bully Free Program at www.bullyfree.com /free-resources/facts-about-bullying. Bullying behaviors have been described as either direct or indirect. A few examples of these behaviors are:

Direct Bullying Behaviors (Physical/Verbal)

Physical bullying means:

- hitting, kicking, slapping, elbowing, shouldering (slamming someone with your shoulder), or pushing someone . . . or even just threatening to do it
- shoving in a hurtful or embarrassing way
- cramming someone into his or her locker
- making someone do things he or she doesn't want to do
- restraining

- pinching
- flushing someone's head in the toilet
- attacking with spit wads or food
- taking, hiding, stealing, damaging or defacing belongings or other property.

Verbal bullying means:

- name-calling
- insulting remarks and put-downs
- racist or bigoted remarks or other harassment with words
- whispering behind someone's back, starting or spreading rumors with the intention to harm or embarrass
- repeated teasing
- threats and intimidation.

Indirect Bullying Behaviors (Social/Relational)

Relationship bullying means:

- refusing to talk to someone
- gossiping, spreading nasty and malicious rumors and lies about someone
- excluding someone from a group or making someone feel left out or rejected (social rejection or isolation)
- destroying and manipulating relationships (turning your best friend against you)
- destroying status within a peer group
- destroying reputations
- humiliating and embarrassing
- intimidating
- spreading hurtful graffiti
- stealing boyfriends or girlfriends to hurt someone
- using negative body language (facial expressions, turning your back to someone) to hurt feelings or undermine confidence
- using threatening gestures, taunting, pestering, insulting remarks and gestures
- glaring and giving dirty looks, telling nasty jokes, passing notes around, anonymous notes
- writing or signing hate petitions (promising to hate someone).

Cyberbullying Behaviors

Cyberbullying can be direct bullying and/or indirect bullying behavior that includes negative messages sent or posted via

- text messages on cell phones and other electronic devices
- email
- chat rooms
- digital photos
- voice mail messages
- Web pages
- social media sites.

Bullying occurs when any of these behaviors is done to another person more than once and usually repeated several times over a period of time.

As teachers we need to help students gain insight into the behaviors and attitudes of bullies. Understanding why an action takes place may be an important step toward preventing, or at least avoiding, the behavior.

So who bullies? And who gets bullied? And what about those who witness, but do nothing?

Coloroso (2011) identifies three consistent players in episodes of bullying and one additional potential player. These players include the bully, the bullied, the bystander, and the potential for a fourth who becomes "the antithesis of the bully. . . . This character can appear in three different and vital roles—those of resister, defender and witness. He or she actively resists the tactics of the bullies, stands up to them and speaks out against their tyranny. The fourth character might also defend and speak up for those who are targeted" (52).

The bystander plays a much more significant role than anyone realizes. By being a witness and doing nothing, a bystander becomes a complicit character whose lack of action diminishes the worth of the victim, empowers and emboldens the bully, and, simply put, makes matters worse. This suggests the need to develop empathy among bystanders, to empower them with strategies of positive action and support for victims.

Swearer, Espelage, and Napolitano (2009) report there is "convincing evidence that students do not remain 'fixed' in the dichotomous roles of 'bully' and 'victim.' In fact, these labels have proven to be problematic in the search for effective bullying prevention and intervention. Too often, adults and students want to punish the bullies or blame the victims. The mind-set of 'once a bully, always a bully' or 'once a victim, always a victim' only serves to keep us stuck in thinking that these are fixed traits in individuals" (1). Although these roles may ebb and flow or even shift over time, Swearer, Espelage, and Napolitano cite evidence that students who are aggressive in elementary school tend to be among the aggressors in middle and high school.

Research suggests that bullies are more likely than peers to experience conduct problems, be delinquent, and become involved in drug or alcohol use. Students who bully tend to exhibit the need to dominate others, to demand they get their own way; they are more likely to exhibit impulsive behaviors and are more easily angered. In addition, students who bully are more often defiant and aggressive toward adults and tend to show little or no empathy for the victims of bullying behaviors.

Olweus (2011) notes that students who bully others are more likely to:

◉ get into frequent fights
◉ steal and vandalize property
◉ drink alcohol and smoke
◉ report poor grades
◉ perceive a negative climate at school
◉ carry a weapon.

Further, Olweus notes that "[n]ot all students who bully others have obvious behavior problems or are engaged in rule-breaking activities, however. Some of them are highly skilled socially and good at ingratiating themselves with their teachers and other adults. This is true of some boys who bully but is perhaps even more common among bullying girls. For this reason it is often difficult for adults to discover or even imagine that these students engage in bullying behavior."

How can we tell if a student is being bullied? What are the signs to look for?

If you suspect someone you know is being bullied here are a few warning signs to watch for (www.stopbullying.gov).

A child is likely the victim of bullying if he or she:

◉ comes home with damaged or missing clothing or other belongings
◉ reports losing items such as books, electronics, clothing, or jewelry

- has unexplained injuries
- complains frequently of headaches, stomachaches, or feeling sick
- has trouble sleeping or has frequent bad dreams
- has changes in eating habits
- hurts themselves
- is very hungry after school from not eating their lunch
- runs away from home
- loses interest in visiting or talking with friends
- is afraid of going to school or other activities with peers
- loses interest in school work or begins to do poorly in school
- appears sad, moody, angry, anxious, or depressed when they come home
- talks about suicide
- feels helpless
- often feels like they are not good enough
- blames themselves for their problems
- suddenly has fewer friends
- avoids certain places
- acts differently than usual.

Why don't victims speak up?
Why don't they seek our help?

School culture has taught children that telling is tattling and has many children convinced that telling anyone would only make matters worse. Beane (2009) offers these as possible reasons victims and bystanders remain silent:

- They believe telling someone is wrong.
- They believe nothing will be done or perhaps nothing can be done to help.
- They fear that adult intervention will make the situation worse.
- They are embarrassed.
- They feel shame in not being able to stand up for themselves.
- They do not want to worry their parents.
- They fear losing friends.

Coloroso (2009) adds that students in a bystander role may not step up because:

- The bully is their friend.
- It's not their problem.
- The victim is not their friend.
- The victim is a loser.
- The victim deserves to be bullied, or asked for it, or had it coming.
- Bullying will toughen the victim up.
- It's better to be part of the in-group than to defend the "outcasts."
- It's too big a pain in the brain.
- Kids have a deeply embedded code of silence. No one wants to be called a "snitch."

We must ensure that schools are places where children feel both physically and emotionally safe. They must feel free to report. Toward that end, we need to teach children the difference between tattling and reporting. "Tattling is telling an adult about another kid's actions with the one and only aim of getting that child into trouble. Reporting is telling an adult about another child's action in order to get help with difficult circumstances" (Dosani 2008, 31).

So what do we do? How can we help? Where do we begin to end bullying?

As Swearer, Espelage, and Napolitano (2009) explain, "We live in a society where punishment-based strategies are often the first line of defense against students' behavioral problems. A student bullies someone else, and we want to see that 'bully' punished for his or her behaviors." However, recent research suggests that punishment-based strategies such as zero tolerance, expulsion, or suspension may not be the most effective reaction. Swearer, Espelage, and Napolitano contend that zero tolerance strategies "should be reserved only for the most severe aggressive and disruptive behaviors. Against this backdrop, we argue that students involved in bullying need to be taught relationship enhancement skills instead of being ostracized and punished for their lack of skills" (95).

So we begin day one with a new group of students coming together in a new year. We work with them, among them, to build community and establish relationship skills, build empathy, redirect their leadership skills in positive channels.

Perhaps it is useful to think of the classroom/school community as a garden. And as in any garden there are occasional weeds that find a way in. To do nothing could result in weeds growing out of control, taking over the garden, and destroying the flowers you have so carefully nurtured. To poison the weed(s) may endanger other healthy plants. Instead, let's work to keep the garden lush and healthy, leaving the weeds no chance for the nourishment they need to thrive. To be clear with this analogy it is the bullying *behavior* and not the student who bullies that we view as the weed. So we are not suggesting the removal of the student; rather, that we focus our attention on nurturing the positive aspects of all students, to empower each of them to recognize and support one another in ways that build community for all to thrive.

CHAPTER 1

Working Toward Kindness, Civility, and Human Compassion as an Integral Part of the Curriculum

It's very dramatic when two people come together to work something out. It's easy to take a gun and annihilate your opposition, but what is really exciting to me is to see people with differing views come together and finally respect each other.

– Fred Rogers

Build Community First

Our profession is coming to understand that bullying is more complex than most of us have previously thought. There are no quick fixes, no set of rules or regulations that will magically turn this around. The research we have read suggests the need to build empathy throughout the community, to highlight and strengthen the bonds of common humanity, to feed and support kindness behavior, and to avoid feeding bullying behaviors through apathy, laughter, and increased social status.

We believe the single most important thing we can teach our children is kindness. And that focus on kindness includes developing respect for humanity and a fervent belief in protecting the dignity of their fellow human beings. In short, community building is essential. Ralph Peterson (1992) reminds us that "community in itself is more important to learning than any method or technique. When community exists, learning is strengthened—everyone is smarter, more ambitious, and productive. Well-formed ideas and intentions amount to little without a community to bring them to life" (2). And there is no better time to begin than the first day of school.

Excitement, tension, worry, perhaps even anxiety build in those days leading up to the new school year. Students are eager to read their names on a list posted for all to see. But finding your name on a list with others does not make an automatic community. Nor are the names on this list neighbors who have chosen to move in and share geography. Students rarely, if ever, have any voice in where they are placed or who else will join them in the new class. So it is unrealistic to expect instant friendships, mutual respect, or the honest caring for others in those first days. That level of caring and trust takes time and effort. It takes intentional actions, deliberate community building, and the development of shared routines, rituals, and ceremonies embedded in most groups and organizations. "The strength of a learning community is the ability of the members to accept one another as they are and to help one another make changes they value. . . . The persistent challenge for teachers is to create a place where members not only come together but also tolerate multiple perspectives" (Peterson 1992, 33).

One known antidote to bullying behavior is the development of healthy social relationships found in a caring community. We must work together to develop the bonds, the trust, the mutual respect, and the self-respect necessary to create community. Peterson (1992) contends this must be an essential focus:

> The primary goal at the beginning of a new year or term is to lead students to come together, form a group, and be there for one another. At first students are concerned foremost with their own welfare. It is by establishing values of caring and trust in the classroom that social ties and interest in one another's welfare comes into existence. Making meaning requires students to be responsible for their own learning, collaborate with others, and learn from their failures as well as their successes. Students don't need to be in agreement with one another, but they do need to see themselves as being responsible for others and find value in group life. The teacher takes the lead in making him- or herself into a trusted person. (13)

Bullying behavior is less likely to emerge in classrooms where all students feel valued, a sense of belonging, and significant to the community. The behavior is typically a manifestation of an individual's lack of empathy for others, a need to feel superior, or a feeling of being better than others perceived as different. Therefore, a careful look at the learning community must be a top priority of schools if we are to prevent unhealthy beliefs and actions of students that will manifest as bullying behaviors.

In his blog on the Developmental Studies Center Web site (2011), Peter Brunn wrote, "We see bullying as an important issue to uncover because it's often a symptom of a larger problem with a school's community and the relationships among students and between students and teachers." This suggests there is a larger problem than the exhibited behavior, and that problem is likely not under the child's control. Rather, the root of the bullying behavior lies in the home, the community, and the school in that child's life.

The International Bullying Prevention Association (www.stopbullyingworld.org) recommends that both the social climate of the school and the social norms in the school and community must be addressed with regards to bullying behavior. Such an effort requires a unified front involving all personnel in the school (i.e., administrators, teachers, assistants, guidance counselors, librarians, specialists, school nurses, custodians, bus drivers, cafeteria workers, etc.) as well as community members, parents, and students.

A healthy learning community must extend beyond the physical walls of the school. We, those of us who work in education, recognize the powerful influence of home, extended family, and civic community in the development of a child's respect for himself and others. Although the school has a significant role to play, we cannot ignore the fact that the family helps a child recognize himself as a member of the greater human family and to recognize there are differences within the scope of humanity. The attitudes and values children develop about those differences begin in their families and neighborhoods. Write a letter to parents, guardians, or caregivers to keep them informed about your plans and to enlist their support (a sample letter is included in Appendix B).

The goal here is to develop a learning community that is both physically and emotionally safe, a place where students trust and respect one another, and a place where the adults demonstrate trust and respect all day, every day with everyone. In short, we are striving to create what the research-based Caring School Community program (Developmental Studies Center) describes as a culture of kindness. "In a caring school community, a culture of kindness and respect permeates each classroom and the entire school. Students are treated warmly, and staff members, parents, and other adults in the school are treated as valued, contributing members of the school community" (DSC Leadership Guide 2009, 2).

So this work begins by building community first. Toward that end we have included a sample antibullying contract for students and assembled a sample collection of community-building activities for those first weeks (see Appendices C and D). Please note there is no order or hierarchy here, so think of the list as a menu of options. Select those that best fit the needs of your group and remember the purpose of these activities is for each individual to come to know others, and to be known as a human being.

Working Toward Kindness, Civility, and Human Compassion

Knowing that we want to lead children to a level of awareness about bullying, let's begin with the more general understandings and move inward toward the specific. It may be helpful to think of this process as moving inward through a series of five concentric circles; a slice of onion is the image that comes to mind. The outer circles represent the most general information, and the inner circles represent the most specific. Those more specific inner circles assume the understandings, insights, ideas, and language acquired through experience with the outer layers. So we move into the deeper insights through exposure, conversation, and repeated opportunities to know and be known as valued members of the human family (see Figure 1.1).

The first of the five layers is focused on discovering how people on the globe are more alike than different and developing a conscious awareness of those things that make us human. The second layer is focused on recognizing that within the family of humanity there are differences. The third layer is dedicated to understanding that dif-

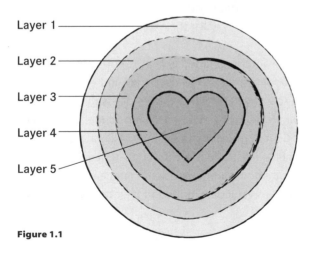

Layer 1
Layer 2
Layer 3
Layer 4
Layer 5

Figure 1.1

The outer circles represent the most general information while the inner circles represent the most specific information. Those more specific inner circles assume the understandings, insights, ideas, and language acquired through experience with the outer layers.

ferences exist; yet how we respond to them is inextricably connected to our beliefs, thoughts, and feelings about difference. The fourth layer is devoted to developing the understanding that as human beings we are more alike than different. Yet, within the scope of humanity there are differences, and those differences make us neither less than nor better than another. They simply make us different. We work toward developing the critical understanding that all human beings are equally valuable and deserve dignity and respect. When some people feel either threatened or superior by the differences of others, their behavior may result in unkind, even harmful actions. The fifth and final layer is devoted to accepting that each of us is responsible for our thoughts, attitudes, and actions. And, as members of the human family, we each have dignity and worth. In addition, we each have a responsibility to protect the human dignity of all others.

The Common Core Standards/College and Career Readiness Anchor Standards (2011) for Reading require that students comprehend as well as critique. Toward this end, it is expected that students are engaged, open-minded—but discerning—readers and listeners. They work diligently to understand precisely what an author or speaker is saying, but they also question an author's or speaker's assumptions and premises and assess the veracity of claims and the soundness of reasoning (2011, 7).

Within each of the five layers of this process, students pause to question and ponder the "bumper sticker" (focus or big ideas) for each book. By the end of the layer, they are developing the overarching "bumper sticker" (thread or central theme) for the set of books, gaining the insights needed to move into the next layer.

Common Core Standards/College and Career Readiness Anchor Standards for Reading (2011) also expect students to come to understand other perspectives and cultures. "Students appreciate that the twenty-first-century classroom and workplace are settings in which people from often widely divergent cultures and who represent diverse experiences and perspectives must learn and work together. Students actively seek to understand other perspectives and cultures through reading and listening, and they are able to communicate effectively with people of varied backgrounds. They evaluate other points of view critically and constructively. Through reading great classic and contemporary works of literature representative of a variety of periods, cultures, and worldviews, students can vicariously inhabit worlds and have experiences much different than their own" (2011, 7).

A key component of this project is leading children to value others, to recognize differences without losing sight of our common humanity. The clear focus of Layer 1 is to acknowledge our common humanity, to see ourselves as one member of the greater human family while recognizing each exists within a time period, culture, community, and family.

The Standards also value evidence. "Students cite specific evidence when offering an oral or written interpretation of a text. They use relevant evidence when supporting their own points in writing and speaking, making their reasoning clear to the reader or listener, and they constructively evaluate others' use of evidence" (2011, 7). As students move with their teacher through each set of books and reach the end of a layer, they construct the lens through which the next layer of books will be viewed. Assumptions are tested and weighed against evidence from the previously read books and new expectations are set for the next layer.

The Standards place focus on results rather than means. "By emphasizing required achievements, the Standards leave room for teachers, curriculum developers, and states to determine how those goals should be reached and what additional topics should be addressed. Thus, the Standards do not mandate such things as a particular writing process or the full range of metacognitive strategies that students may need to monitor and direct their thinking and learning. Teachers are thus free to provide students with whatever tools and knowledge their professional judgment and experience identify as most helpful for meeting the goals set out in the Standards" (2011, 4).

We have chosen to work through a multilayered approach, examining the big ideas and central themes stretching across a thoughtfully and intentionally selected set of books. The behaviors, feelings, thoughts, and motives of characters are closely examined. Insights, thoughts, and theories are used to move inward and to go deeper, working toward generalizations and specific personal understandings.

Moving through the five layers of complexity via focused read aloud experiences and guided conversations, students are given opportunities to engage in the following College and Career Readiness Anchor Standards for Reading (2011, 10):

Key Ideas and Details

1. Read closely to determine what the text says explicitly and to make logical inferences from it, cite specific textual evidence when writing or speaking to support conclusions drawn from the text.

2. Determine central ideas or themes of a text and analyze their development, summarize the key supporting details and ideas.

3. Analyze how and why individuals, events, and ideas develop and interact over the course of a text.

Craft and Structure

4. Interpret words and phrases as they are used in a text, including determining technical, connotative, and figurative meanings, and analyze how specific word choices shape meaning or tone.

5. Analyze the structure of texts, including how specific sentences, paragraphs, and larger portions of the text (e.g., a section, chapter, scene, or stanza) relate to each other and the whole.

6. Assess how point of view or purpose shapes the content and style of a text.

Integration of Knowledge and Ideas

7. Integrate and evaluate content presented in diverse media and formats, including visually and quantitatively, as well as in words.

8. Delineate and evaluate the argument and specific claims in a text, including the validity of the reasoning as well as the relevance and sufficiency of the evidence.

9. Analyze how two or more texts address similar themes or topics in order to build knowledge or to compare the approaches the authors take.

Range of Reading and Level of Text Complexity

10. Read and comprehend complex literary and informational texts independently and proficiently.

Through a selection of trade books read to and with students, adults can help students carefully and objectively examine the behaviors of bullies, the bullied, and bystanders (as witness resister or defender). Through a series of guided read aloud experiences, adults can help children closely examine the archetypical characters and situations most often associated with incidents of bullying. Through read aloud experiences followed by conversations focused on the behaviors and motives, feelings and emotions, situations and settings portrayed in literature (trade books and mass media), children can begin to develop understanding and insight.

Getting to Know the Layers and Essential Understandings

The books and lessons are presented in a series of five layers. Each layer, designed to guide students toward specific insights and understandings, serves as the scaffolding for the next and are organized as shown in Figure 1.2.

LAYER 1	LAYER 2	LAYER 3

GETTING STARTED: We Have So Much in Common

Essential Understandings

- As human beings, we are more alike than different.
- Those things that make each of us human are present in every other human across the globe.

Featured Titles

- *Whoever You Are* (1997) by Mem Fox
- *Skin Again* (2004) by bell hooks
- *We Share One World* (2004) by Jane E. Hoffelt
- *All the Colors of the Earth* (1994) by Sheila Hamanaka
- *Same, Same but Different* (2011) by Kostecki-Shaw

MOVING IN: There Are Ways in Which We Are Different—Not Less Than Others, Not Better Than Others, Just Different

Essential Understandings

- Within the range of humanity, there are differences.
- Some differences are more obvious than others.
- The differences that exist within the range of humanity do not make any of us more human or less human.
- Any difference or combination of differences does not alter the fact that we are all human and does not take away any of the aspects we all share as members of the human family.
- A difference does not make another human better than others or less than others; a difference merely makes us different.

Featured Titles

- *Ian's Walk* (1998) by Laurie Lears
- *Mama Zooms* (1993) by Jane Cowen-Fletcher
- *Moses Goes to a Concert* (1998) by Isaac Millman
- *The Pirate of Kindergarten* (2010) by George Ella Lyon
- *The Colors of Us* (1999) by Karen Katz

INSIDE THE CIRCLE: Thinking, Feeling, Acting

Essential Understandings

- Our actions reflect our beliefs and feelings, our thoughts and values.
- How we treat other people shows what we believe about ourselves and our relationship to other human beings.
- Unkind behavior toward another person shows a sense of feeling more important or less important than others.

Featured Titles

- *Be Good to Eddie Lee* (1993) by Virginia Fleming
- *Bee-Wigged* (2008) by Cece Bell
- *Hooway for Wodney Wat* (1999) by Helen Lester
- *Odd Velvet* (1998) by Mary E. Whitcomb
- *Camp K-9* (2011) by Mary Ann Rodman

Figure 1.2

LAYER 4	LAYER 5

AT THE CORE: When Others Are Not Thoughtful, Caring, and Kind

Essential Understandings

- People who do not think of all others as fellow human beings can learn to appreciate difference.
- People who do not see others equally worthy of dignity and compassion can come to understand the power of kindness.
- People who think differences make one person more worthy or more important than another person can learn that no one is more important than another.
- People who are unkind or intentionally harmful to another human being can learn to change their beliefs and their behaviors.

Featured Titles

- *Bootsie Barker Bites* (1992) by Barbara Bottner
- *Dog Eared* (2002) by Amanda Harvey
- *The Recess Queen* (2002) by Alexis O'Neill
- *The Bully Blockers Club* (2004) by Teresa Bateman
- *Bully* (2001) by Judith Caseley

GETTING FOCUSED FOR ACTION: An Opportunity to Explore the Actions of Others, Reflect on Our Own Feelings, and Redirect Our Behaviors Toward Fellow Human Beings

Essential Understandings

- I am responsible for my thoughts and feelings.
- I am responsible for my actions.
- I am responsible for the way I treat others.
- I choose to be a bystander or a defender when others are being bullied.
- I am enough; I do not succumb to the attempts of others to build themselves up by making me feel intimidated or lessened.
- I am enough; I do not need to make others feel lessened in order to feel that I am enough.
- Making someone else feel bad does not make me feel better.
- Making someone else frightened does not make me feel powerful and important.
- I am part of the human family.
- Everything that makes me human is present in all other people.
- I respect myself and I think and act accordingly.

Featured Titles

- *Stand Tall, Molly Lou Melon* (2001) by Patty Lovell
- *Hey Little Ant* (1998) by Phillip and Hannah Hoose
- *A Chance to Shine* (2006) by Steve Seskin and Allen Shamblin
- *One* (2008) by Kathryn Otoshi
- *Those Shoes* (2007) by Maribeth Boelts

The Lessons: Read Alouds and Guided Conversations

We begin moving through the layers with read aloud experiences using thoughtfully selected picture books. Although many books could be appropriate for each layer, we have identified a small set of books that we have found particularly useful. If these books are not available to you, select books with a similar message or theme that will help your students develop the essential understandings of that layer. At the end of this book (see Appendix A), we have included an extensive list of additional titles sorted by layer.

As you begin working with each layer, we recommend that you and your class study at least three to five books depending upon the time you are able to devote. The understandings and insights developed through the focused read aloud experiences are essential to the practice of kindness and empathy, and to the peaceful, ethical treatment of others. An essential factor in these experiences is developing the understanding that each human being is worthy of basic dignity and human compassion. Students will learn that as an individual you are enough, your worth does not lie in the opinions or approval of others, and that you do not garner personal worth by attacking the worth of others.

We recommend that for each of the five layers you work with three to five books over ten to fifteen days. This means that you may return to each title up to three times. The schedule for a single book may look something like this:

DAY 1

- ◉ Opening conversation
- ◉ Visual tour/reading the art
- ◉ Read aloud
- ◉ Brief discussion after the read aloud
- ◉ Generating a bumper sticker
- ◉ Personal reflections (written or art)

DAY 2

- ◉ Revisiting the bumper sticker
- ◉ Sharing reflections from day 1
- ◉ Noting the connections (or lack of connection) between the bumper sticker and the reflections
- ◉ Repeating the read aloud

- Stretching your thinking, sketching/writing about your insights, revising the bumper sticker if necessary
- Personal action goal ("Now that we have read this book and thought about what it means for our community I will try to . . .")

DAY 3

- Revisiting the bumper sticker
- Sharing sketches, reflections, and personal action goals

We have attempted to include titles with a range of complexity, so we encourage you to preview the featured titles. If you find a particular title too simple for your class, simply select an alternate title from the appendix. We intentionally layer in flexibility to give you options.

You may find that your students need only one visit with a few titles. Their comments, bumper stickers, and action statements will reveal your students' thinking and insights. In this case, you may choose to move on to the next book or select an additional title from the appendix.

If you are thinking about the amount of time needed, this may help you get a clearer picture of what it takes to work through the five layers:

3 books per layer	15 books total	1–3 visits per book	15–45 days
4 books per layer	20 books total	1–3 visits per book	20–60 days
5 books per layer	25 books total	1–3 visits per book	25–75 days

Remember that each visit involves the development of literacy skills/strategies, opportunities for conversation, critical thinking, comparison/contrast, character analysis, reflection, and more. It will help children gain the insights and language needed to confront and neutralize the behaviors of bullies, in themselves and in others.

CHAPTER 2

Getting Started
We Have So Much in Common

*As different as we are from one another, as unique as each
one of us is, we are much more the same than we are different. That may be the most essential message of all, as we
help our children grow toward being caring, compassionate,
and charitable adults.*

– Fred Rogers

Working Through Layer 1

I t is our belief that the most basic understanding necessary for engaging in the ethical treatment of others is to recognize what is common among all human beings.
Until children come to understand that other people living in a nearby city, across
the country in another state, or in a country across the globe have all aspects of humanity in common, it will be difficult to move forward.

The purpose of Layer 1 is to lead children toward the development of those basic
concepts and to help them develop the language to articulate their understandings
and insights. Some children have more difficulty naming or articulating the common-
alities shared by all humans than noticing the differences. We have chosen picture
books that make our shared humanity the focus. It is necessary to be well grounded in

these essential understandings if we hope to have young people recognize the humanity in all others.

Open this layer with a general conversation about people. Choose a larger, well-known city in your region and ask your students to think about this: "Are people in (name your city or town) the same as people in (name the larger city)? Are we different from them? Are there ways we are like them or different from them? Just think. If you say we are alike, think about examples of how we are alike. If you say we are different, think about examples of how we are different."

The idea here is to get them thinking. Some children will go immediately to the idea that we are alike in some ways and different in others. Other children will see some similarities and focus on the ways people in two locations in the same region are alike. But many children will begin with the differences, or perceived differences.

Allow a short amount of time for them to think, share their thoughts with a partner, and then report to the group. Make no comments that could be perceived as validation or negation of their ideas, simply repeat the thinking, "So far you are thinking . . ."

Push their thinking a bit further. Choose a foreign country with high visibility (China, for example) and pose the same question. "Are there ways that people in our town are like people in a faraway place such as China? Are there ways we are different? Are there ways we are like them and different from them? Think for a few moments. If you say we are alike, think about examples of how we are alike. If you say we are different, think about examples of how we are different."

Once again, allow a short amount of time for them to think, share their thoughts with a partner, and then report to the group. Make no comments that could be perceived as validation or negation of their ideas.

In each situation, summarize their ideas and examples. Now move on to the first book in Layer 1 and begin with the Visual Tour/Reading the Art.

Layer 1 in Action: Day 1

While developing the layers and selecting books, we visited a few schools in Decatur, Alabama, to work with students in kindergarten through fifth grades. During this process Lester introduced the read aloud of *Whoever You Are* with each group in a very similar way:

Opening Conversation

Lester: Before we read this book, I'd like us to think about Birmingham and the people who live there. Birmingham is not too far away, but we don't go there very often. And Birmingham is a much bigger place than your town, right?

[Everyone nods in agreement.]

Lester: Are people in Birmingham like us or different from us? Are there ways we are the same? Think about that.

[I pause about thirty seconds for thinking.]

Lester: Take a few seconds to tell your partner what you are thinking. If you think of ways we are different, tell your partner how we are different. If you think of ways we are the same or alike, tell your partner how we are alike.

[I pause about forty-five seconds for sharing.]

Lester: I can tell you had a lot of thoughts about this idea. Let's hear from a few of you. Would you tell us something your partner told you, please?

[I pause about forty-five seconds for sharing.]

Lester: Now I'm going to stretch your brain a bit. I want you to think about people in a place that is very far away from here, someplace like China. Think about people in China. And think about people here. Are we different from them? Are there ways we are the same as people in China? Let's sit with those thoughts for a moment. That's a lot to think about.

[I pause about thirty seconds for thinking.]

Lester: Now tell your partner what you are thinking. And listen to your partner's thoughts as well.

[I pause about forty-five seconds for sharing.]

Lester: We have a lot of thinking going on. Let's hear from a few of you. Would you tell us something your partner told you, please?

Kindergarten:

> My eyes are a different color from them.
>
> Their eyes look like this (pulls at the corner of her eyes).
>
> They put, um, chopsticks in their hair in China.

Lester: So you think people in China are different from us? Tell me any ways we are the same as people in China.

Kindergarten:

> We got the same shoes.
>
> We all like football stuff.
>
> All of us wear clothes but they might not be the same color.
>
> We all got feelings.

Lester: So we can be like other people in some ways and different from them in other ways. Is that correct?

[Most children nod in the affirmative.]

Visual Tour/Reading the Art

Lester: Let's take a look at this book, *Whoever You Are*. It is written by Mem Fox and the illustrator is Leslie Staub. Take a look at the cover. This man is holding four children. They are flying around something. What is that circle they are flying around?

Kindergarten: The world. The earth.

Lester: It is the earth and what are all these little dots on the earth? Look closely, what those are?

Kindergarten: Lots of kids standing on the earth. They are watching him fly.

Lester: I'm wondering why that man would fly those children all around the world. What would he want them to notice?

Kindergarten: He wants them to see all the boys and girls all over the world.

Lester: Hmm. Perhaps that is what he has in mind. Let's take a look at the pages inside. As we turn the page, we can see everyone up close; perhaps the man is going to take those children on a journey. And did you notice all those houses? On the next page, the man and the four children are flying across the sky. And here in the center is another little girl. Notice all the houses again, even on her dress.

Kindergarten: All the houses are the same. They are the same on her dress, too.

Lester: And here the girl with houses on her dress is standing in the middle of the world; other children are all around her smiling. Their skin is different colors, and their hair is different colors, and they are in different places on the world, but they share the same world. And the sun shines on all of them and the moon is there for each of them all over the world. Think about that for a moment. Let's pause to look at this page and think a little longer.

Kindergarten: They all live in the world, but they got different color skin like us. Yeah, we don't have the same color. Some of us are black and some is white and some of us is mixed.

Lester: On this page the man and the four children are standing on top of this building. It seems they are going around the world searching. We can see different kinds of houses and we can see four children up close. Notice how they are the same—they each have a nose and eyes and a smile and hair and skin and they all live together on one earth.

Kindergarten: We have a nose and two eyes. Everybody has a nose. But some people's eyes are a different color. My eyes are brown, everybody in my family's eyes are brown but my brother. He has green eyes. His eyes are beautiful.

Lester: I'm thinking this book is helping us see all the ways we are alike, even if we are different in some ways. On this page there is a group of children.

Kindergarten: They're at school. Yeah, but it's not like our school. They all wear the same kind of clothes. And they are reading those boards. We don't read boards. We got books in our room.

Lester: Yes, these children are reading something different from our books and their school looks different from ours. But, they are in school just like us. Hmm, I think I am getting an idea from this book. Take a look. These children are riding a donkey. What do we ride to get where we are going?

Kindergarten: Cars! We ride on the school bus. I ride on my bike.

Lester: Let's think about that. These children are riding a donkey and they are wearing clothes that are very different from ours. But they are doing their work and taking care of the animals just like us. The flying man and the four kids are seeing children all over the world. What do you suppose he wants them to understand?

Kindergarten: We all wear clothes. Children go to school everywhere in the world.

Lester: We are getting some big ideas from thinking about these illustrations. On this page a family has a cart of vegetables. In the hills we can see rows of crops growing. They have vegetables and fruits in very large baskets. Perhaps this is where they buy food.

Kindergarten: We buy food at the grocery store. And Wal-Mart. We go to Kroger.

Lester: Now the flying man is looking in the window at a child and a mom in a rocking chair. I wonder what he wants us to think about.

Kindergarten: Moms rock their babies all over the world. And grandmas, too. Moms love babies.

Lester: Take a look at these pages. We see three people with big smiles here and on this page three boys laughing at the monkey on one boy's head.

Kindergarten: 'Cause people smile and laugh all over the world. I would laugh if you had a monkey on your head.

Lester: We are getting big ideas from reading the art. I'm wondering what big message we are going to get when we read the words. Let's take a look at this next page. Two people are waving good-bye, they are crying. That bus is filled with people and luggage. Why do you suppose they are crying?

Kindergarten: Because they are leaving their family. I would cry if I had to leave my family. He is sad. They don't want to go. He wants to go with them.

Lester: Do you suppose that people all over the world feel sad when someone in their family is leaving for a while?

Kindergarten: Yes, everybody all over the world. It's sad when you leave.

Lester: Look, the flying man is holding a birthday cake. There are lots of birthday cakes all around him. I suppose people all over the world have birthdays, eh? This girl is grown up now and she is a doctor. And these people look like the four kids all grown up.

Kindergarten: Everybody grows up all over the world. And that one has a baby. Yeah, she's writing a note. You can grow up and be anything you want. Like that girl is a doctor. She was a little girl and she "growed" up to be a doctor.

Lester: Let's turn the page. There are four people with cuts and bandages and drops of blood. Their skin is different colors, but look at the blood. What do you notice about the blood?

Kindergarten: If you get a cut, you get blood. Blood is red. It don't matter what color your skin is, everybody's blood is the same. Everybody's blood is red on the inside.

Lester: And the little boy in the center is holding his knee and crying.

Kindergarten: It hurts if you get cut. And we cry no matter how big we are.

Lester: This book is helping us think about important ideas. Let's look at the last pages and think about the message there. Here's a group of people and it looks like the children are back with their families. Everyone is waving and smiling and hearts are falling like rain-drops. And over here the flying man is dropping hearts on every-one. Then on this last page the flying man has a string of hearts circling the earth.

Kindergarten: He is dropping love on everybody. 'Cause everybody needs love all over the world. You need love when you are sad and if you get cut.

Lester: We have read the art on every page and now we have some ideas about the big message in this book. We have noticed that there are children all over the world who have friends and families, that people all over the world laugh and cry and play. We noticed that people all over the world have houses and food and work. People all over the world are alike in many ways, no matter where they live.

Read Aloud

Lester: Let's go back to the beginning and read the words this time. I'm going to read all the way through without stopping. Think about what you noticed when we read the art and listen for new ideas. Remember, we can always go back to any page if you have something to say after we finish the book. Listen now as I read.

[I read the book in a slow, deliberate pace with attention to meaningful phrasing. I occasionally pause to draw attention to the ways we are all alike as members of one human family.]

After the Read Aloud

Lester: Remember, readers and writers are people who think, so let's take a moment to think about this book. After we read the art, we were thinking about all the ways people are alike all over the world. Mem Fox also gives us a message with her words. Let's just pause and think about that for a moment. What is the message of this book?

[I allow a period of silence.]

Lester: Would you share your thinking with your partner now, please?

[I allow about forty seconds.]

Lester: Now let's hear what your partners shared with you.

Kindergarten:

We all fall and get hurt.

We all bleed when we get cut.

We all have to go to doctors.

We all need food.

Children can't go places without their momma.

Children get hungry everywhere.

We need to be kind to people even in Florida and Texas.

We can share and we can help them get back to their spot.

We can play nice.

No matter where you live, everybody needs love.

Everybody got red blood no matter where you live.

Lester: Now let's take a look at our list. [I read through the list, noticing aloud how there is overlap.] On another day, you and your teacher will visit this book again. I'd like you to try to come up with a "bumper sticker" that can say one big message from this book.

As we play with each other and work with each other, let's be mindful of the messages in this book. Let's promise to remind each other about all the ways we are like people all over the world.

NOTE: Comments from older children, though more sophisticated, follow a similar pattern. Prior to the Visual Tour/Reading the Art and read aloud, their comments tended to go to the obvious differences. Following the read aloud, the comments moved to exploring our common humanity.

NOTE: The idea of a "bumper sticker" for each book helps move the thinking toward big ideas within the layer. We find it helpful to have a conversation about bumper stickers to set up the expectation. When everyone is gathered in the circle, show the group an appropriate bumper sticker. The one we like to use features a drawing of the globe in the center being embraced by two arms. The caption reads, "Love Your Mother." Read the bumper sticker to the group and give them time to think about the message. Then with a puzzled look on your face, ask, "Hmm, I wonder what this means? What is this message asking us to do?" Children almost always go immediately to the core of this message with comments like, "Take care of the earth, Mother Earth. Get it?" Ask them for examples of how we can do that. Typical responses include a list of conservation tips: turn off the lights, don't litter, don't pollute, recycle, compost, plant a garden. Connect this insight to the work ahead: "Wow, all those ideas are in that one small bumper sticker? I wonder if we could read this whole book and come up with a bumper sticker to remind us what messages are here. Let's give that a try. Listen as I read . . . ."

Essential Understandings for All Books in Layer 1:
- As human beings, we are more alike than different.
- Those things that make each of us human are present in every other human across the globe.

LAYER 1: BOOK 1 (*WHOEVER YOU ARE*)

Title: *Whoever You Are*

Author: Mem Fox

Illustrator: Leslie Staub

1997, 2001 Voyager Books ISBN 0–15–216406–5

This simple text, with vibrant illustrations attending to the nuances of meaning, will focus attention to the ways each of us is like every other human across the globe.

DAY 1: INTRODUCE THE BOOK

VISUAL TOUR/READING THE ART

Present the book so that it is visible to everyone. Tell your students what you would like them to focus on. Then slowly move through the images. Point out a few subtle details as examples of those aspects that may build meaning.

As we view the art I'd like you to look for:

- evidence of the many different ways each of us is like every other person in the world
- details included in the art that cause you to wonder or have a question.

As we view the art I'd like you to think about:

- why this man in the blue suit is flying these children around the world
- what these children are seeing as they travel with the man
- what these children may be thinking as they travel from place to place
- what this may mean and what we should listen for when we read the text.

READ ALOUD

Read the book aloud with careful attention to pacing, tone, intensity, and mood. Let your voice convey the essence of the text. Read the complete text without stopping.

As I read I'd like you to listen for:

- evidence of how each of us is the same as every other person in the world
- evidence of how life may be different in other places in the world.

As I read I'd like you to think about:

- what this means to you
- any messages you think the book has for us
- ideas you would like to talk about
- a bumper sticker (the big message) for the book.

AFTER THE READ ALOUD

Close the book and sit with the language for a few seconds. Resist the urge to tell your students what they are supposed to understand. Sit in silence and expect them to do the same. After ten to fifteen seconds, speak in a quiet voice to gently move the conversation forward.

- **Think on your own:** *Let's pause here and think about the meaning of this book. What does this text suggest for you?* [Think/Write]
- **Stretch your thoughts with a partner:** *Now let's take about forty-five seconds to think together. Talk quietly with your partner, listen to your partner's ideas, share your thoughts, and think of a bumper sticker for this book.* [Share/Expand]
- **Share your new thinking:** *Let's share a few of your bumper stickers.* [Collaborate/Synthesize]

DAYS 2–3: EXTEND THIS THINKING UNTIL THE NEXT BOOK

Option 1: Have students get to know their classmates. Using an icebreaker exercise, find ways each student is like three other classmates. Search for ways beyond the obvious ones (two eyes, two hands, etc.).

Option 2: Create a bulletin board with cells for family, favorite food, hobbies, and so on.

Option 3: Chart the ways we are all alike in our class.

Option 4: Reflect and write: *What will you try to do differently now that we have shared this experience?*

LAYER 1: BOOK 2 (*SKIN AGAIN*)

Title: *Skin Again*

Author: bell hooks

Illustrator: Chris Raschka

2004 Jump at the Sun (Hyperion) ISBN 0–7868–0825–X

On the surface, this is a very simple book about race, though it can be the springboard to important conversation. Through minimal text and lively art, this book reminds us that skin is merely the wrapper we arrive in and what truly counts is within us. Yet another reminder of how, as human beings, we are more alike than different.

DAY 1: INTRODUCE THE BOOK

VISUAL TOUR/READING THE ART

Present the cover, making sure the art is visible to everyone. Tell your students that the text in this book is large, bold, and very visible. Assure them that you will return to the text and read the book aloud after you examine the art. Remind them that their focus at this point is to closely examine the art, to look with attention to detail, thinking about what the art conveys. Encourage them to think about what the artist may want viewers to think about. As you move slowly through the pages, pause at selected points to allow them to think about what they have seen and what the images are evoking for them.

As we view the art I'd like you to look for:

- images of a snake, an onion, and a heart shape that Chris Raschka includes
- examples of how the artist draws our attention to contrasts
- details used by the artist to help us see how we are alike and different.

As we view the art I'd like you to think about:

- why the artist chose those specific images
- how we can be alike, but also different.

READ ALOUD

Read the book aloud with careful attention to pacing, tone, intensity, and mood. Let your voice convey the essence of the text. This is a simple text with a big message; take your time. Read the complete text without stopping.

As I read I'd like you to listen for:

- examples of the ways we can get to know a person
- reasons why we can't really know someone just by their skin.

As I read I'd like you to think about:

- how the words written by bell hooks sparked the images made by Chris Raschka
- the idea that skin is just the "wrapper" we come in
- what things really matter about a person
- what things make no difference
- what are those things that make each of us the same
- what is the message this book holds for us
- a bumper sticker (the big message) for the book.

AFTER THE READ ALOUD

Close the book and sit with the language for a few seconds. Resist the urge to tell your students what they are supposed to understand. Sit in silence and expect them to do the same. After ten to fifteen seconds, speak in a quiet voice.

- **Think on your own:** *Let's pause here and think about the meaning of this book. What does this text suggest for you?* [Think/Write]
- **Stretch your thoughts with a partner:** *Now let's take about forty-five seconds to think together. Talk quietly with your partner, listen to your partner's ideas, share your thoughts, and think of a bumper sticker for this book.* [Share/Expand]
- **Share your new thinking:** *Let's share a few of your bumper stickers.* [Collaborate/Synthesize]

DAYS 2–3: EXTEND THIS THINKING UNTIL THE NEXT BOOK

Option 1: Bring a bag of identical individually wrapped candy (peppermints, Hershey Kisses, etc.) and count out enough for each student to have one. Equally distribute the candy in four identical boxes. Wrap each box in four different types of wrapping paper ranging from newspaper to gift wrap. Place the four wrapped boxes in a location where they are highly visible as the children enter the classroom.

Gather the class in a circle and return to the book. Revisit the bumper stickers from the previous visit with the book and place the four boxes in the center of the circle. Tell the group: "I brought a small treat for each of you today. Each box has the same treat inside, but notice how the boxes look different on the outside. The only difference is the paper, or 'the skin,' each is in. So if you get to choose, will it matter which box your treat comes from?" Pause here and let them think about the connection to the book. Encourage conversation about how we sometimes make decisions based on the "wrapping" without knowing what's inside. Then, of course, open the boxes and enjoy.

Option 2: Reflect and write: *Let's make a page in our notebook for this book. Continue thinking about the ideas from this book and what the candy boxes help us think about. Jot down your thoughts on your Skin Again page. Look for ways we can see this happening not just with the candy boxes but also with people we have met.*

Option 3: Reflect and write: *What will you try to do differently now that we have shared this experience?*

LAYER 1: BOOK 3 (*WE SHARE ONE WORLD*)

Title: *We Share One World*

Author: Jane E. Hoffelt

Illustrator: Marty Husted

2004 Illumination Arts ISBN 0–9701907–8–6

Through the eyes and thoughts of one young boy, we visit children across the globe, attending to the many ways we share one world as members of one human family. Though the text is simple and the art portrays some stereotypes of the lands and cultures visited, the book does provide an opportunity for thinking about the essential understandings.

DAY 1: INTRODUCE THE BOOK

VISUAL TOUR/READING THE ART

Present the book so that it is visible to everyone. Tell your students what you would like them to focus on. Then slowly move through the images. Point out a few subtle details as examples of those aspects that may build meaning.

As we view the art I'd like you to look for:

- evidence of how each of us is like every other person in the world
- the boy in the corner of each page (Notice what he is doing and how it is very much like what other children in other parts of the world do as well.)
- details included in the art that cause you to wonder or have a question.

As we view the art I'd like you to think about:

- ways the message in this book is like the message in *Whoever You Are* by Mem Fox
- the message these illustrations send to you
- what this boy notices and understands as he looks in on the lives of other children around the world
- what this may mean and what we should listen for when we read the text.

READ ALOUD

Read the book aloud with careful attention to pacing, tone, intensity, and mood. There is very minimal text in this book. Don't rush. Move slowly, allowing children to concentrate and take in all the detail in the art while thinking about the single focus in the text of each page. Note the cumulative effect of the single focus on each spread and revisit all we share in this one world as you reach the end.

As I read I'd like you to listen for:

- evidence of how each of us is like every other person in the world
- the ways life may be different in other places in the world, yet we have so much in common.

As I read I'd like you to think about:

- what this means to you
- any messages you think the book has for us
- ideas you would like to talk about
- a bumper sticker (the big message) for the book.

AFTER THE READ ALOUD

Close the book and sit with the language for a few seconds. Resist the urge to tell your students what they are supposed to understand. Sit in silence and expect them to do the same. After ten to fifteen seconds, speak in a quiet voice.

- **Think on your own:** *Let's pause here and think about the meaning of this book. What does this text suggest for you?* [Think/Write]
- **Stretch your thoughts with a partner:** *Now let's take about forty-five seconds to think together. Talk quietly with your partner, listen to your partner's ideas, share your thoughts, and think of a bumper sticker for this book.* [Share/Expand]

- **Share your new thinking:** *Let's share a few of your bumper stickers.* [Collaborate/Synthesize]

DAYS 2–3: EXTEND THIS THINKING UNTIL THE NEXT BOOK

Option 1: Get to know your community. Explore the idea that your class shares one community [classroom for K–1 children, school for grades 2–3, neighborhood/town/city for grades 4–5] and consider all the ways individuals may bring diversity while the group shares so much in common.

Option 2: Launch a campaign for awareness and collect evidence of the ways we share our community (as defined above).

Option 3: Reflect and write: *What will you try to do differently now that we have shared this experience?*

LAYER 1: BOOK 4 (*ALL THE COLORS OF THE EARTH*)

Title: *All the Colors of the Earth*

Author: Sheila Hamanaka

Illustrator: Shelia Hamanaka

1994 Mulberry Books/Morrow ISBN 0–688–17062–5

This lyrical, poetic text is brief and focused. Paired with rich oil paintings, the language gently reminds us that color is everywhere in the world and that love (and people) come in all colors.

DAY 1: INTRODUCE THE BOOK

VISUAL TOUR/READING THE ART

Present the book so that it is visible to everyone. Tell your students what you would like them to focus on. Then slowly move through the images. Point out a few subtle details as examples of those aspects that may build meaning.

As we view the art I'd like you to look for:

- evidence of the many ways color is part of the world around us
- examples of how all our skin tones are found in the world around us
- details included in the art that cause you to wonder
- any ways we are all alike.

As we view the art I'd like you to think about:

- the message the illustrator seems to present
- how the message in this book is like the message in *Whoever You Are* by Mem Fox
- what this may mean and what we should listen for when we read the text
- any questions the art makes you want to ask.

READ ALOUD

Read the book aloud with careful attention to pacing, tone, intensity, and mood. There is very minimal text in this book. The language is rhythmic and poetic. Move slowly, allowing children to hear the comparisons and concentrate and take in all the detail in the art while thinking about the bigger message.

As I read I'd like you to listen for:

- evidence of the many ways color is a beautiful part of the world around us, even in the people we know
- the many beautiful ways people can be different and still be part of the human family.

As I read I'd like you to think about:

- what this means to you
- any messages you think the book has for us
- ideas you would like to talk about
- a bumper sticker (the big message) for the book.

AFTER THE READ ALOUD

Close the book and sit with the language for a few seconds. Resist the urge to tell your students what they are supposed to understand. Sit in silence and expect them to do the same. After ten to fifteen seconds, speak in a quiet voice.

- **Think on your own:** *Let's pause here and think about the meaning of this book. What does this text suggest for you?* [Think/Write]
- **Stretch your thoughts with a partner:** *Now let's take about forty-five seconds to think together. Talk quietly with your partner, listen to your partner's ideas, share your thoughts, and think of a bumper sticker for this book.* [Share/Expand]
- **Share your new thinking:** *Let's share a few of your bumper stickers.* [Collaborate/Synthesize]

DAYS 2–3: EXTEND THIS THINKING UNTIL THE NEXT BOOK

Option 1: Explore the comparisons made in the book between people and the world around them. Examine those same connections in the classroom, school, or civic community. Initiate a conversation around what these insights can mean for the ways we think and behave within our community. Invite their thoughts on the implications for how we treat one another within our community (classroom, school, civic, world).

Option 2: Reflect and write: *What will you try to do differently now that we have shared this experience?*

LAYER 1: BOOK 5 (*SAME, SAME BUT DIFFERENT*)

Title: *Same, Same but Different*

Author: Jenny Sue Kostecki-Shaw

Illustrator: Jenny Sue Kostecki-Shaw

2011 Henry Holt ISBN 978–0805089462

Two young boys become pen pals exchanging both letters and drawings. Elliot, who lives in America, and Kailash, who lives in India, recognize how much their lives are the same even though there are obvious differences. There is a focus on family and play, home and food, and school. The boys begin to comment how they are the "same, same but different."

DAY 1: INTRODUCE THE BOOK

VISUAL TOUR/READING THE ART

Present the cover, making sure the art is visible to everyone. The art in this book represents the lives of two boys. One lives in America and the other lives in India. On the cover we see both boys. Rotate the book so each is seen clearly.

Think about the title, Same, Same but Different, *and think about what we have learned from the other books we have studied in this layer. Remember, we have been thinking that no matter where people live, or what they look like, or what they eat, or how they celebrate, people are still human beings just like us. We are all alike in so many ways, even if some things in our lives are different. This book invites us to notice how one boy in America and one boy in India are the same but different. Let's have a look.*

As we view the art I'd like you to look for:

  * examples of what the artist does to help us see how the characters are different

- examples of what the artist does to help us see how the characters are alike
- evidence of the message you think the artist wants us to think about.

As we view the art I'd like you to think about:

- how we can be both the same and different.

READ ALOUD

Read the book aloud with careful attention to pacing, tone, intensity, and mood. As you read, remember this is an exchange of letters between two boys. Let your voice reflect the rhythm and intonation of that exchange.

As I read I'd like you to listen for:

- examples of the ways we can get to know another person
- how two people in different parts of the world can have much in common
- what the two boys learned about each other.

As I read I'd like you to think about:

- why people around the world have so much in common
- what are those things that make each of us the same
- what is the message this book holds for us
- a bumper sticker (the big message) for the book.

AFTER THE READ ALOUD

Close the book and sit with the language for a few seconds. Resist the urge to tell your students what they are supposed to understand. Sit in silence and expect them to do the same. After ten to fifteen seconds, speak in a quiet voice.

- **Think on your own:** *Let's pause here and think about the meaning of this book. What does this text suggest for you?* [Think/Write]
- **Stretch your thoughts with a partner:** *Now let's take about forty-five seconds to think together. Talk quietly with your partner, listen to your partner's ideas, share your thoughts, and think of a bumper sticker for this book.* [Share/Expand]
- **Share your new thinking:** *Let's share a few of your bumper stickers.* [Collaborate/Synthesize]

DAYS 2–3: EXTEND THIS THINKING UNTIL THE NEXT BOOK

Option 1: Over the next several days, begin to notice and make note of the ways we are the same, same but different in the classroom and in the school. Expand this to include a larger worldview for older students. Encourage them to observe the comparisons/contrasts on news, in life, in their reading, and so on.

Option 2: Set up digital pen pals with students in other classrooms within the school, with a class from another school within the district, or with a class from another state or region of the country. As a class, collect digital photos and video clips to exchange. Keep a class journal (or chart) of the ways students in your class and the pen pals are the same, same but different.

Option 3: Reflect and write: *What will you try to do differently now that we have shared this experience?*

CHAPTER 3

Moving In

There Are Ways in Which We Are Different— Not Less Than Others, Not Better Than Others, Just Different

The world needs a sense of worth, and it will achieve it only by its people feeling that they are worthwhile.
–Fred Rogers

Working Through Layer 2

You have spent several days developing the central ideas in Layer 1:

- As human beings, we are more alike than different.
- Those things that make each of us human are present in every other human across the globe.

These essential understandings become the scaffolding upon which you will build the next insights and concepts. Each of the books in Layer 2 will feature one character that is different in some way (autism, skin color, hearing loss, visual impairment, traditions, etc.). In this layer we are working with a set of books, wearing the lens of Layer 1, reminding ourselves that each human being possesses all that makes any one of us human. As we introduce each book in Layer 2, we revisit the essential understandings of Layer 1 and explore differences that exist within the human family.

The purpose of Layer 2 is to lead children toward understanding that differences exist within the human family, that some of those differences may be physical and visible to the eye, while some may be noticed in other ways. However, no difference makes anyone more or less human. So in this layer we explore books that feature difference and celebrate the difference without losing sight of the common bonds of our humanity.

Layer 2 in Action: Day 1

We visited classrooms to get reactions to the ideas in Layer 2. In each classroom, Lester sat on the floor and gathered the students around him in a circle. To introduce the essential understandings from Layer 1, Lester used *Whoever You Are* by Mem Fox and proceeded through an experience similar to the one described with kindergarten students. Then he moved to *Ian's Walk* by Laurie Lears with a group of fourth and fifth graders.

Opening Conversation

Lester: We all agree that people everywhere on the globe are like us in many ways. Yet, we noted many ways that people are different, right? [Students nod in agreement.] We agreed that what makes each of us human is present in every other person on earth no matter where they live, or how they live, or what they do differently. You said no difference makes one of them better than anyone else, or not as good as any other person. Do you still think that? [Students nod in agreement and mumble some affirmative comments.]

Visual Tour/Reading the Art

Lester: Now I want to show you another book called *Ian's Walk: A Story About Autism*. It is written by Laurie Lears and illustrated by Karen Ritz. Take a look at the cover. The boy featured here is Ian and the girl on the cover is his older sister, Julie. Notice that Ian is looking up into the trees as he walks down the sidewalk. Julie walks closely behind; notice where her eyes are focused.

[I continue to guide students through the illustrations by drawing their attention to the contrast between the portrayal of Ian and all the other characters in the art. Students make comments along the way.]

Read Aloud

[I read the text aloud, pausing to explore connections between the language and what students notice in the art.]

After the Read Aloud

Lester: I'd like you to think for a moment about our insights from *Whoever You Are*. We have noticed a few ways Ian is different. We noted how that makes Julie feel sometimes, but I'd like us to think about all the ways Ian is like every other person in the world. Let's just pause and think about that for a bit. [We sit in silence for about thirty-five seconds.] Thank you. Now use those thoughts and decide if Ian's difference makes a difference. Does his difference make Ian less human than other people? Does it change how valuable and important he is in the world? Let's sit with that for a bit. [Again there is silence for about thirty-five seconds.] Thank you, now I'd like you to share your thinking with the person next to you. In just a moment, I'll ask you to share with the group.

Fourth Grade—Ian's Walk:

We hear the same sounds but react differently.

We all have a brain but it is different in some people or children with special ways.

We are all human.

Some people have a good attitude and some people or children have a bad attitude [referring to how others treat someone with an observable difference].

We should treat him as we want to be treated.

Don't say he is dumb, just say he is different.

We shouldn't let others' likes and dislikes bother us.

People are just people wherever you go.

Friends should stick up for friends.

Fifth Grade—Ian's Walk:

Ian is living and he has the same blood as everybody else.

Ian has a soul just like every other person.

We are all human beings, we just react differently to things.

I knew a boy one time who had his legs amputated and people made fun of him.

One time I had to go to speech and people made fun of me . . . my friend stood up for me.

My parents were proud of me when I stood up for my friend.

Sometimes people laugh and tease someone who is different, but we should remember they are still people just like us.

Picking on others makes you look bad.

Essential Understandings for All Books in Layer 2:

- Within the range of humanity, there are differences.
- Some differences are more obvious than others.
- The differences that exist within the range of humanity do not make any of us more human or less human.
- Any difference or combination of differences does not alter the fact that we are all human and does not take away any of the aspects we all share as members of the human family.
- A difference does not make another human better than others or less than others; a difference merely makes us different.

LAYER 2: BOOK 1 (*IAN'S WALK*)

Title: *Ian's Walk: A Story About Autism*

Author: Laurie Lears

Illustrator: Karen Ritz

1998 Albert Whitman & Company ISBN 0–8075–3480–3

Julie and her older sister Tara want to go to the park. Their little brother Ian wants to go as well. Their mother reluctantly agrees and reminds the girls they will need to watch him closely because he has autism. The morning at the park provides readers/ listeners an opportunity to explore the world through the lens of a child with autism and a glimpse into the emotions of his siblings.

DAY 1: INTRODUCE THE BOOK

VISUAL TOUR/READING THE ART

Present the book so that it is visible to everyone. Draw attention to the art. Begin with the cover illustration, noting the sister, her hands in her pockets, is walking behind the smaller (perhaps younger) brother. Her eyes are watching him. His head is tilted back and his eyes are fixed on something above him. He seems to not be watching where he is going.

As we view the art I'd like you to look for:

- examples of how Ian does things differently from any of the other characters in the art
- examples of how other characters react to Ian
- examples of what Ian has in common with every other human on the globe.

As we view the art I'd like you to think about:

- how the sisters support Ian
- what Ian teaches his sisters
- what seems to fascinate Ian
- how Ian is very much like every other person.

READ ALOUD

Read the book aloud with careful attention to pacing, tone, intensity, and mood. Let your voice convey the essence of the text. Read the complete text without stopping.

As I read I'd like you to listen for:

- examples of how Ian responds to others
- examples of how Ian explores the world
- examples of how Ian's mom and sisters react to him
- examples of things most people would notice, but Ian seems to ignore

- examples of what most people think a little boy would want to do in the park
- examples of what the sisters do instead.

As I read I'd like you to think about:

- whether we can respect and be friends with people who are different from us
- whether we can learn from people who are different from us
- whether it makes a person more important or less important when they are different from us.

AFTER THE READ ALOUD

Close the book and sit with the language for a few seconds. Resist the urge to tell your students what they are supposed to understand. Sit in silence and expect them to do the same. After ten to fifteen seconds, speak in a quiet voice.

- **Think on your own:** *Let's pause here and think about the meaning of this book. What does this text suggest for you?* Allow about forty seconds for this. [Think/Write]
- **Stretch your thoughts with a partner:** *Now let's take about forty-five seconds to think together. Talk quietly with your partner, listen to your partner's ideas, share your thoughts, and think of a bumper sticker for this book.* [Share/Expand]
- **Share your new thinking:** *Let's share a few of your bumper stickers.* [Collaborate/Synthesize]

DAYS 2–3: EXTEND THIS THINKING UNTIL THE NEXT BOOK

Option 1: *Let's begin by thinking about ourselves. I have two things for you to think about across the next several days. Make notes or lists in your log as you reflect and observe over the next few days.*

- *I am like every other person because . . . .*
- *I am different from some people because . . . .*

Option 2: *Today we will return to* Ian's Walk. *We have thought about how we can be both different from others and the same as others. We've made lists of our own differences and talked about how those differences are just part of who we are. As we read through* Ian's Walk *this time, I'd like you to notice Ian's ways of doing things. Notice what captures his attention and how that may be different from most other people. I've made a chart to* *help us make note of our thoughts. When we reach the end of the book I'd like you to share your observations. Then let's think together about all the ways Ian is like every other person in the world.*

Ian's Way of Doing Things	What Most Other People Do

Identify all the ways Ian is like every other person in the world.

LAYER 2: BOOK 2 (*MAMA ZOOMS*)

Title: *Mama Zooms*

Author: Jane Cowen-Fletcher

Illustrator: Jane Cowen-Fletcher

1993 Scholastic ISBN 0–590–45775–6

Our narrator is a young boy whose mom is in a wheelchair that he calls her "zooming machine." Through their interactions and his imagination, we are given a glimpse of living with difference. The wheelchair is fully visible in only a few scenes, partially exposed in some, and not visible at all in several.

DAY 1: INTRODUCE THE BOOK

VISUAL TOUR/READING THE ART

As we view the art in this book, we will meet a little boy who is the narrator. We don't know his name. We also meet his mom and they love to play and pretend.

As we view the art I'd like you to look for:

- the hats and toys on the title page and watch for them throughout the book
- examples of how the little boy and his mom are just like us and most other people (Guide them to notice behavior as well as physical examples.)
- examples of any differences.

As we view the art I'd like you to think about:

- how the hats and toys help us know the boy is pretending with his mom
- what message the art has for us
- how the mom, the boy, and the dad are like all the people we know
- how this mom is like most moms
- how this mom is different from most moms
- whether the differences we can see make any person more or less important than the others.

READ ALOUD

Read the book aloud with careful attention to pacing, tone, intensity, and mood. Read the complete text without stopping.

As I read I'd like you to listen for:

- all the ways this little boy and his mom play and pretend
- examples of how this mom is like most other moms
- examples of how this mom is different from most other moms.

As I read I'd like you to think about:

- how this mom may have to do things differently
- whether this difference keeps her from being a mom
- whether this difference changes the way she feels about her little boy
- whether this difference changes the way the little boy feels about his mom
- the many ways we can be different from each other
- how differences can be more than what is visible
- whether these differences make anyone in the story more or less important than others.

AFTER THE READ ALOUD

Close the book and sit with the language for a few seconds. Resist the urge to tell your students what they are supposed to understand. Sit in silence and expect them to do the same. After ten to fifteen seconds, speak in a quiet voice.

- **Think on your own:** *Let's pause here and think about the meaning of this book. What does this text suggest for you?* Allow about forty seconds for this. [Think/Write]
- **Stretch your thoughts with a partner:** *Now let's take about forty-five seconds to think together. Talk quietly with your partner, listen to your partner's ideas, share your thoughts, and think of a bumper sticker for this book.* [Share/Expand]
- **Share your new thinking:** *Let's share a few of your bumper stickers.* [Collaborate/Synthesize]

DAYS 2–3: EXTEND THIS THINKING UNTIL THE NEXT BOOK

Option 1: *Over the next several days think about other ways people can be different. Make a list of those in your notebook. Each time you list something, pause to remember the mother in this book and write about how that difference influences how the person may look or behave. Then reflect on what we have learned and decide if that difference makes a person more important than others, less important than others, or just the same as others. Let's talk about that in a few days.*

Option 2: Reflect and write: *What will you try to do differently now that we have shared this experience?*

LAYER 2: BOOK 3 (*MOSES GOES TO A CONCERT*)

Title: *Moses Goes to a Concert*

Author: Isaac Millman

Illustrator: Isaac Millman

1993 Scholastic ISBN 0–374–45366–7

Moses and his classmates are deaf. Their teacher takes the class to a concert where the percussionist is also deaf. Readers learn how both deaf and hearing children can enjoy this musical performance.

DAY 1: INTRODUCE THE BOOK

VISUAL TOUR/READING THE ART

Begin with the cover and draw attention to the group of children entering the theatre. Point out that the boy facing us must be Moses, the main character. He is holding a program so he will know who the performers are.

Pause a moment to explore all the obvious ways Moses is like the other children.

As we view the art I'd like you to look for:

- details that may give you clues about how Moses is different from many other people
- details that show how that difference is noticed by others
- examples of how Moses and his class do things differently
- the small boxes with extra illustrations that are added to several pages.

As we view the art I'd like you to think about:

- what those small boxes with extra illustrations are for and what they help us to know about ourselves and about Moses
- how it would feel to be going to a concert in a big theatre with a large crowd of other children and teachers
- how it would feel to be in that large crowd if you were very different from most of the other people going in
- how you would want other people to treat you at the concert.

READ ALOUD

Read the book aloud with careful attention to pacing, tone, intensity, and mood.

As I read I'd like you to listen for:

- examples of how Moses and his classmates participate in the concert
- examples of how Moses and his class do things just like you
- examples of how deaf people can enjoy music.

As I read I'd like you to think about:

- different ways people can enjoy a concert and music
- what we can learn from Moses and his friends
- what we can learn from the musicians, especially the percussionist
- why the teacher gives each child in his class a balloon to hold during the concert
- whether a difference can make a person more important or less important than us.

AFTER THE READ ALOUD

Close the book and sit with the language for a few seconds. Resist the urge to tell your students what they are supposed to understand. Sit in silence and expect them to do the same. After ten to fifteen seconds, speak in a quiet voice.

- **Think on your own:** *Let's pause here and think about the meaning of this book. What does this text suggest for you?* Allow about forty seconds for this. [Think/Write]
- **Stretch your thoughts with a partner:** *Now let's take about forty-five seconds to think together. Talk quietly with your partner, listen to your part-*

ner's ideas, share your thoughts, and think of a bumper sticker for this book. [Share/Expand]

- **Share your new thinking:** *Let's share a few of your bumper stickers.* [Collaborate/Synthesize]

DAYS 2–3: EXTEND THIS THINKING UNTIL THE NEXT BOOK

Option 1: *Let's begin by thinking about ourselves. I have two things for you to think about across the next several days. Make notes or lists in your log as you reflect and observe over the next few days.*

- *Do I know anyone who is deaf or hearing impaired?*
- *What will I do differently now that I have thought about hearing impairment or hearing loss as only a difference within the human family?*
- *Think about all the things you know by sound. Is there any other way to know those things? How would you know about them if you could not hear?*

I know the sound of: Water splashing	How could I know about that if I could not hear? I could feel the droplets or see it moving
Identify all the ways a person with a hearing impairment is like every other person in the world.	

Option 2: Let's explore how each of us has differences. The first step is to think about what our differences are. We will take a few moments each day to talk about what you are noticing and reflecting on.

LAYER 2: BOOK 4 (THE PIRATE OF KINDERGARTEN)

Title: *The Pirate of Kindergarten*

Author: George Ella Lyon

Illustrator: Lynne Avril

2010 Atheneum/Richard Jackson Books ISBN 978–1416950240

Ginny has undiagnosed double vision that has her bumping into chairs and reading the same line twice in reading circle. Classmates laughed and Ginny didn't realize that all the others didn't see two of everything. She did notice if she closed one eye she saw only one, but her teacher told her not to squint. During a vision screening, the nurse discovers that Ginny is seeing double and lets her know most people only see one. A visit to the eye doctor, eye exercises, glasses, and a temporary eye patch do the trick. The illustrations are engaging and a few scenes give the reader a glimpse of what it is like to have double vision.

DAY 1: INTRODUCE THE BOOK

VISUAL TOUR/READING THE ART

Present the book so that it is visible to everyone. Proceed through the pages slowly, and draw attention to those scenes where double images are portrayed.

As we view the art I'd like you to look for:

- clues to what makes Ginny different
- clues to how that difference shows up in Ginny's life
- examples of how Ginny has to do some things differently
- anything in the art that makes you wonder.

As we view the art I'd like you to think about:

- how Ginny is feeling
- how others can help or hurt when they notice the difference of another person
- how Ginny's difference changes the way she act and feels
- how Ginny is very much like every other person.

READ ALOUD

Read the book aloud with careful attention to pacing, tone, intensity, and mood. Let your voice convey the subtle shifts in emotion to highlight Ginny's feelings as she keeps a good attitude and works hard to do her best.

As I read I'd like you to listen for:
- examples of how Ginny sees things differently
- examples of what Ginny thinks and feels about seeing double
- examples of how others help Ginny or treat her unkindly.

As I read I'd like you to think about:
- how Ginny sees the world is a bit different from the way most of us see
- what we can learn from Ginny's experience
- what we can learn from her teacher and the nurse and the eye doctor
- whether it makes people more important or less important when they are different from us.

AFTER THE READ ALOUD

Close the book and sit with the language for a few seconds. Resist the urge to tell your students what they are supposed to understand. Sit in silence and expect them to do the same. After ten to fifteen seconds, speak in a quiet voice.

- **Think on your own:** *Let's pause here and think about the meaning of this book. What does this text suggest for you?* Allow about forty seconds for this. [Think/Write]
- **Stretch your thoughts with a partner:** *Now let's take about forty-five seconds to think together. Talk quietly with your partner, listen to your partner's ideas, share your thoughts, and think of a bumper sticker for this book.* [Share/Expand]
- **Share your new thinking:** *Let's share a few of your bumper stickers.* [Collaborate/Synthesize]

DAYS 2–3: EXTEND THIS THINKING UNTIL THE NEXT BOOK

Option 1: *Let's begin by thinking about ourselves. I have two things for you to think about across the next several days. Make notes or lists in your log as you reflect and observe over the next few days.*

* *How is my view of the world different from that of many other people?*
* *Who do I know that wears glasses or contacts or has a vision impairment?*
* *Talk with that person about what the world looks like without their glasses.*

What is life like for people who can't see clearly?	How is that different for others who can?

Identify all the ways a person with a visual impairment is like every other person in the world.

Option 2: *Let's explore how each of us has differences. The first step is to think about what our differences are. We will take a few moments each day to talk about what you are noticing and reflecting on.*

LAYER 2: BOOK 5 (*THE COLORS OF US*)

Title: *The Colors of Us*

Author: Karen Katz

Illustrator: Karen Katz

2007 Henry Holt ISBN 978–0805081183

Lena, a seven-year-old artist, is painting portraits of friends and neighbors. Her mother, also an artist, explains how to mix colors to find the right shade for each of the people in the neighborhood. In the process Lena discovers all the colors of us.

DAY 1: INTRODUCE THE BOOK

VISUAL TOUR/READING THE ART

As we view the art in this book, notice all the different colors and skin tones of human beings. Lena is the main character here and she is learning how to mix colors. Let's take a look.

As we view the art I'd like you to look for:

- the various colors and skin tones
- all the colors of paint Lena has in her room
- examples of differences other than skin color among the people in this story.

As we view the art I'd like you to think about:

- why the author/illustrator is showing all these different people
- why the color of skin is the focus of the art
- how all these people are alike
- whether the differences we can see make any person more or less important than the others.

READ ALOUD

Read the book aloud with careful attention to pacing, tone, intensity, and mood. Read the complete text without stopping. Read in a smooth and calm tone with a steady pace that allows students to take in the connection between the colors of us and the colors of things in our world.

As I read I'd like you to listen for:

- examples of what Lena learns about color and skin tone
- examples of how Lena's mom helps her think about the shades of brown
- examples of what Lena learns on the walk.

As I read I'd like you to think about:

- how skin color or tone is just one part of us
- the many ways we can be different from each other
- how differences can be more than what is visible
- whether these differences make anyone in the story more or less important than others.

AFTER THE READ ALOUD

Close the book and sit with the language for a few seconds. Resist the urge to tell your students what they are supposed to understand. Sit in silence and expect them to do the same. After ten to fifteen seconds, speak in a quiet voice.

- **Think on your own:** *Let's pause here and think about the meaning of this book. What does this text suggest for you?* Allow about forty seconds for this. [Think/Write]
- **Stretch your thoughts with a partner:** *Now let's take about forty-five seconds to think together. Talk quietly with your partner, listen to your partner's ideas, share your thoughts, and think of a bumper sticker for this book.* [Share/Expand]
- **Share your new thinking:** *Let's share a few of your bumper stickers.* [Collaborate/Synthesize]

DAYS 2–3: EXTEND THIS THINKING UNTIL THE NEXT BOOK

Option 1: *Let's begin by turning to this page (return to the dedication page) with all these different hands around the edges. Take a moment and think about two things.*

- *How are all these hands alike?*
- *What makes these hands different?*

Chart the similarities and differences identified by the students.

Option 2: *Now let's explore our hands. In your group take a look at the hands of each person and think about these two things:*

- *How are all our hands alike?*
- *What are the differences?*

Guide them to notice more than skin tone. Chart the similarities and differences identified within the groups.

Option 3: *This week let's think about the people we see in our school every day. Let's think about the colors of us the way Lena and her mom did on their walk. Remember how Lena and her mom thought of foods and spices and things from nature to describe the colors of skin in their neighborhood. Let's try to think of ways to describe the colors of us.*

As you observe and think about this, you may want to revisit Skin Again *by bell hooks, a book we read earlier.*

What are the colors of the people in our school?	What do each of them have in common with all other people?
Teacher	
Principal	
Custodian	
Secretary	
Librarian	
Art teacher	
Physical ed. teacher	
Music teacher	

CHAPTER 4

Inside the Circle
Thinking, Feeling, Acting

Anything that's human is mentionable, and anything that is mentionable can be more manageable. When we can talk about our feelings, they become less overwhelming, less upsetting, and less scary. The people we trust with that important talk can help us know that we are not alone.
—Fred Rogers

Working Through Layer 3

As you transition into Layer 3, challenge your students to take the essential understandings from the first two layers and synthesize them into a guiding frame for this work. Ask them to reflect on the messages we have built from the books we have shared to this point. You may find it helpful to list these:

- ◉ As human beings, we are more alike than different.
- ◉ Those things that make each of us human are present in every other human across the globe.
- ◉ Within the range of humanity, there are differences.
- ◉ Some differences are more obvious than others.

- ◉ The differences that exist within the range of humanity do not make any of us more human or less human.
- ◉ Any difference or combination of differences does not alter the fact that we are all human and does not take away any of the aspects we all share as members of the human family.
- ◉ A difference does not make another human better than others or less than others; a difference merely makes us different.

Proceed into Layer 3 using these understandings as the frame of reference for developing new insights. We have selected books with an added twist in the plot for Layer 3. In these books you will meet at least one character with a difference that becomes the target of teasing or taunting from another character. Within the context of these books we are working toward developing the insight that we own our feelings toward others. That is, our behaviors and actions toward others are a reflection of our beliefs and feelings, thoughts and values. As a result, the way we treat others shows what we believe about the value of other people and how we value ourselves in relation to other people. In short, unkind behavior toward others reflects a sense of feeling more important than others or being threatened by them in some way.

Layer 3 in Action: Day 1

During Layer 3, a second-grade class meeting centered on the book, *Hooway for Wodney Wat*.

Opening Conversation

Lester: Today we are starting a new layer of books so let's remind ourselves what we have learned from the first two layers. Think about the bumper stickers we made for those.

Second Grade: We are different on the outside but the same on the inside.

Lester: So that's true even for a person with a difference like Ian or Moses [characters from previous books]?

Second Grade: Yes, it's true for everyone.

Visual Tour/Reading the Art

Lester: Today we are going to read and think about this book, *Hooway for Wodney Wat* by Helen Lester with art by Lynn Munsinger. Let's read the art on a few pages before we read the text. Did you notice that all the characters are different kinds of rodents?

Second Grade: Yes. They are rats and mice. That one is a guinea pig.

Lester: Can you tell which one the others are teasing?

Second Grade: It's the little one in the purple jacket. He has his head down. He's holding his tail.

Lester: What are the others doing?

Second Grade: [Laughing] She is sticking out her tongue. They are making fun of him.

Read Aloud

Lester: I will tell you that a big bully is going to show up as a new kid. Notice what happens when she comes in. Let's read the words now. [I read the story using voices to match the attitudes and feelings of the characters.]

After the Read Aloud

Lester: Let's return to the beginning of the book now. What was happening in this book?

Second Grade: They teased him because he couldn't pronounce his *r*'s. He said *w*, like *weed* instead of *read* and *wake* for *rake*.

Lester: So Rodney is different in one way. Does that make him more important or less important than anyone else in his class?

Second Grade: No. He's still like the others on the inside.

Lester: Do the other kids have a right to tease Rodney because he can't pronounce his *r*'s?

Second Grade: [A resounding "no" bounces around the circle.] That's being a bully.

Lester: So what have we learned that Rodney's classmates didn't know yet?

Second Grade: Everyone is the same on the inside, even if they are different on the outside. You don't make friends by teasing other people. That's not kind.

Lester: Let's think about another character now. Let's think about Camilla Capybara. We met Camilla on her very first day in this class. Camilla came in acting like a bully. Can you think of anything that might have happened in her old school that would make her believe she needed to come to this new school and act like a bully?

Second Grade: She was bigger than anyone. Maybe they bullied her in her old school and said she was fat. Yeah, maybe she is thinking she has to come to this school and be a bully before they are mean to her first.

Lester: Wait. I need to think about this. Hmm, you mean if someone is bullied then that person might bully someone else?

Second Grade: Yeah 'cause she don't want to get bullied in the new school.

Lester: Hmm. So if someone is behaving like a bully, they might be a really nice person underneath? You mean they are like us on the inside?

Second Grade: Yes, they are still people . . . different on the outside, but the same on the inside.

Lester: Let's think about this. Imagine that we were in Rodney's class and this new girl, Camilla, came in behaving that way. What could we do to help her understand that we are friends and she doesn't have to behave like a bully here?

Second Grade: We could say, "What if I did that to you? How would you like it?" You could be nice to her. You could say stop it and if she doesn't you could tell the teacher and the teacher will fix it. We could say this is not how we do things in our classroom and I don't like it when you act like that. We could explain that Rodney can't pronounce his *r*'s and tell her what he means.

Lester: It sounds as if we have learned a lot from our other books about how to react if someone behaves like a bully.

Lester: Now let's think about something a little different. Remember the part where Camilla was acting like an airplane and pulling up the weeds around the sign, and screaming at the leaves trying to wake them up? Think about those parts. I remember that we laughed and giggled at Camilla. It was funny in the story, wasn't it? What if Camilla was a new kid in our class and we were laughing like that? Would we be acting like bullies then?

Second Grade: In our room we have a rule that we treat people the way we want to be treated. But when they went outside they were not treating Camilla the way they wanted to be treated.

Essential Understandings for All Books in Layer 3:

- Our actions reflect our beliefs and feelings, our thoughts and values.
- How we treat other people shows what we believe about ourselves and our relationship to other human beings.
- Unkind behavior toward another person shows a sense of feeling more important or less important than others.

LAYER 3: BOOK 1 (*BE GOOD TO EDDIE LEE*)

Title: *Be Good to Eddie Lee*

Author: Virginia Fleming

Illustrator: Floyd Cooper

1993 Philomel ISBN 0–399–21993–5

Summer has finally arrived. The routine of school is left behind and Christy sits on the porch wondering how to spend her time. She notices Eddie Lee on his front steps across the street and remembers her mother saying to be good to him. Eddie Lee, a boy with Down syndrome, seems to be a bother and wants to always tag along, but Christy keeps thinking about her mother's words. When her friend JimBud comes along the two of them ignore Eddie Lee. And when they set off to go wading and search for frog eggs, JimBud is less than kind with his comments and actions toward Eddie Lee. As the story unfolds Christy learns the power of kindness and the meaning of true friendship.

DAY 1: INTRODUCE THE BOOK

VISUAL TOUR/READING THE ART

As we view the art I'd like you to look for:

- the three main characters and think about the ways they are all the same
- how the three main characters are different from one another
- the three characters and think about why we never see them all playing together
- one scene where all three characters are present, but Eddie Lee is isolated (Notice the posture and gestures and facial expressions in that scene. Think about what each character may believe and feel and think in that moment.)
- why Christy, the girl in the book, is with JimBud in the beginning of the book and with Eddie Lee at the end.

READ ALOUD

Read the book aloud with careful attention to pacing, tone, intensity, and mood. One character (JimBud) seems to have a note of sarcasm and disdain in his voice. Let that be heard as you read. Note the shifts in tone or intensity as the story progresses and let that be heard in your voice as well.

As I read I'd like you to listen for:

- what Christy thinks about Eddie Lee and how she feels about spending time with him
- the difference between how she acts/talks with JimBud and with Eddie Lee
- how JimBud and Christy speak to/treat Eddie Lee differently.

As I read I'd like you to think about:

- JimBud's behaviors toward Eddie Lee and what those behaviors show us about his beliefs
- Christy's behaviors toward Eddie Lee and what those behaviors show us about her beliefs.

AFTER THE READ ALOUD

Close the book and sit with the language for a few seconds. Resist the urge to tell your students what they are supposed to understand. Sit in silence and expect them to do the same. After ten to fifteen seconds, speak in a quiet voice.

- **Think on your own:** *Let's pause here and think about the meaning of this book. What does this text suggest for you?* Allow about forty seconds for this. [Think/Write]

  What does Christy understand and believe that is different from the beliefs of her friend JimBud? Can we be friends with others who think and believe differently?

- **Stretch your thoughts with a partner:** *Now let's take about forty-five seconds to think together. Talk quietly with your partner, listen to your partner's ideas, share your thoughts, and think of a bumper sticker for this book.* [Share/Expand]

- **Share your new thinking:** *Let's hear a few of your bumper stickers.* [Collaborate/Synthesize]

DAYS 2–3: EXTEND THIS THINKING UNTIL THE NEXT BOOK

Recall the insights from Layer 1 and Layer 2. Revisit the bumper stickers from those books and have students think about Christy, Eddie Lee, and JimBud. The following questions can frame the written responses arising from conversations initiated in the days between readings:

- *What do we understand?*

- *In this book, Christy's behavior changed. Think about how that happened. Is there a bumper sticker for our brains?*

- *How could we help JimBud, Christy, and Eddie Lee if they were in our class?*

- *Is there any situation where getting to know someone has helped you change your thinking about a person and your behavior toward that person?*

- *What does this story make you think about? What will you do differently now that we have shared this book and these thoughts in our community?*

LAYER 3: BOOK 2 (*BEE-WIGGED*)

Title: *Bee-Wigged*

Author: Cece Bell

Illustrator: Cece Bell

2008 Candlewick ISBN 978–0763636142

Jerry is an enormous bee. He is kind and sincere and generous, but Jerry has no friends. All anyone can see is an enormous bee and fear immobilizes them. Things change when Jerry finds a wig on the sidewalk, puts it on, and is mistaken for a boy on the way to school. With the wig, Jerry's character shines through and he becomes fast friends with everyone. But things quickly change when the wind blows the wig away. Jerry and the others learn a few things about character and friendship and kindness. You will, too.

DAY 1: INTRODUCE THE BOOK

VISUAL TOUR/READING THE ART

As we view the art I'd like you to:
- notice how Jerry Bee is always set apart from the other characters
- think about why that is happening
- notice the posture and expressions of the other characters
- think about what the other characters are thinking and feeling and believing
- notice how Jerry tries to make friends
- notice details that let us know how he feels
- think about Jerry's feelings and beliefs
- notice when the posture and expressions of others begin to change
- think about what causes those changes to occur.

READ ALOUD

Read the book aloud with careful attention to pacing, tone, intensity, and mood. The characters in this book seem to have a note of sarcasm and disdain in their voices. Let that be heard as you read. Note the shift in fonts that signals a shift in tone or intensity.

As I read I'd like you to:

- notice what Jerry wants most of all
- think about details in the language that let us know
- think about how Jerry tries to make friends
- notice how others react and think about why they react this way
- notice what happens to make other characters change
- think about Jerry (Does he change when others do?)
- think about how Jerry is the same with the "wig" and without the "wig"
- notice how other characters react when the "wig" is blown off Jerry's head
- think about what the change in their behavior suggests about what they think and believe.

AFTER THE READ ALOUD

Close the book and sit with the language for a few seconds. Resist the urge to tell your students what they are supposed to understand. Sit in silence and expect them to do the same. After ten to fifteen seconds, speak in a quiet voice.

- **Think on your own:** *Let's pause here and think about the meaning of this book. What does this text suggest for you?* Allow about forty seconds for this. [Think/Write]

  Do we sometimes make up our minds about a person before we even get to know them? How did that happen in this story?

- **Stretch your thoughts with a partner:** *Now let's take about forty-five seconds to think together. Talk quietly with your partner, listen to your partner's ideas, share your thoughts, and think of a bumper sticker for this book.* [Share/Expand]

- **Share your new thinking:** *Let's hear a few of your bumper stickers.* [Collaborate/Synthesize]

DAYS 2–3: EXTEND THIS THINKING UNTIL THE NEXT BOOK

Recall the insights from Layer 1 and Layer 2. Revisit the bumper stickers from those books and have students think about Jerry and his classmates. Initiate conversations connecting this book with the cumulative thinking across the previous books and ask the students to write. Use these prompts:

- *What have we come to understand?*
- *In this book, Jerry was the same before and after the wig. But the behaviors of the other characters were different. Think about why that happened. Is there a bumper sticker for our brains?*
- *Think about any situation where you changed your mind about a person after you got to know them. What changed your thinking? How did that change the way you treat that person? Is there a bumper sticker from the lesson you learned that may help the rest of us?*
- *What will you try to do differently now that we have shared this experience?*

LAYER 3: BOOK 3 (*HOOWAY FOR WODNEY WAT*)

Title: *Hooway for Wodney Wat*

Author: Helen Lester

Illustrator: Lynn Munsinger

1999 Walter Lorraine/Houghton Mifflin ISBN 0–395–92392–1

Rodney, a rodent, has difficulty pronouncing his r's. The other rodents in his class tease and taunt Rodney. He is often isolated and left out. When a new rodent, Camilla Capybara, arrives she becomes the class bully and the group dynamics shift.

DAY 1: INTRODUCE THE BOOK

VISUAL TOUR/READING THE ART

As we view the art I'd like you to:

- notice details in the art that suggest Rodney is different from his classmates
- take a look at the details in the first illustration (Look closely at the books Rodney has around him. Notice the monogram on his pillow.)
- think about what these details reveal about Rodney
- notice the posture and actions of other characters when they are around Rodney
- think about what their posture and expressions suggest about their thoughts and values
- think about what those other characters may be saying to Rodney
- think about how Rodney is feeling

- notice the arrival of a new character (Camilla) and notice how everyone seems to change when she enters
- think about how she is different from all the others and how she is the same
- notice the changes in the faces and expressions of the others when she arrives
- think about what they are feeling and thinking
- think about the message the artist wants to send.

READ ALOUD

Read the book aloud with careful attention to pacing, tone, intensity, and mood. This book has deliberately used invented spelling to allow readers to hear the articulation of a character who has difficulty pronouncing *r*'s. Play with this effect. Note also that Rodney is subjected to the teasing and taunting of his classmates. Be sure to let your voice reflect those shifts.

As I read I'd like you to listen for:

- examples of how Rodney is different
- examples of how Rodney's classmates tease him
- examples of how Rodney reacts to the teasing
- examples of how Camilla is different
- examples of how Camilla acts toward others
- examples of how others react to Camilla's actions and comments.

As I read I'd like you to think about:

- how Rodney feels when others are teasing him
- what the others feel and think about Rodney's difference
- what the words and actions of Rodney's classmates suggest about what they believe about his difference and themselves
- what Camilla believes about herself (What do her words and actions suggest about her thoughts and beliefs?)
- the other classmates and contrast what they say and do to Rodney with what they say and do to Camilla (Think about what these differences reveal to us about their thoughts and beliefs about difference.)

⦿ why Camilla behaves like a bully on her first day in a new school. (What might have happened in her old school that would make her believe that she must be this way at the new school?)

AFTER THE READ ALOUD

Close the book and sit with the language for a few seconds. Resist the urge to tell your students what they are supposed to understand. Sit in silence and expect them to do the same. After ten to fifteen seconds, speak in a quiet voice.

⦿ **Think on your own:** *Let's pause here and think about the meaning of this book. What does this text suggest for you?* Allow about forty seconds for this. [Think/Write]

⦿ **Stretch your thoughts with a partner:** *Now let's take about forty-five seconds to think together. Talk quietly with your partner, listen to your partner's ideas, share your thoughts, and think of a bumper sticker for this book.* [Share/Expand]

⦿ **Share your new thinking:** *Let's share a few of your bumper stickers.* [Collaborate/Synthesize]

DAYS 2–3: EXTEND THIS THINKING UNTIL THE NEXT BOOK

Option 1: Recall the insights from Layer 1 and Layer 2. Revisit the bumper stickers from those books and have students think about Rodney and his classmates. Some things to think and write about over the next few days include:

⦿ *What do we understand now that Rodney's classmates didn't understand in the story?*

⦿ *What could we teach those classmates? How would we do that?*

⦿ *If we had been in Rodney's class what could we have done to make things better?*

⦿ *If we were Rodney's friends how could we help him?*

⦿ *If we were there in the class when Camilla arrives, what could we do that would be kind and wise?*

Option 2:

⦿ Create a pledge or promise for our behavior toward any new student.

⦿ Create a pledge or promise for our reaction to anyone who exhibits bullying behavior.

LAYER 3: BOOK 4 (*ODD VELVET*)

Title: *Odd Velvet*

Author: Mary E. Whitcomb

Illustrator: Tara Calahan King

1998 Chronicle Books ISBN 0–8118–1004–1

On the first day of school all the kids notice that Velvet is . . . odd. She does things differently. She doesn't look or act the same as everyone else. She is just . . . different. As the story unfolds, Velvet's classmates begin to appreciate her.

DAY 1: INTRODUCE THE BOOK

VISUAL TOUR/READING THE ART

As we view the art I'd like you to:

- notice where the main character is placed on the page in relation to all the other characters
- think about what the artist is suggesting about Velvet and how she is treated
- think about what the classmates are thinking and feeling about themselves and about Velvet
- notice Velvet's expressions (Does she seem bothered by the behaviors of the other classmates?)
- notice differences among the other children and think about how those differences either do or do not affect the behavior of any character.

READ ALOUD

Read the book aloud with careful attention to pacing, tone, intensity, and mood. The characters in this book seem to have a note of disdain in their voices. Let that be heard as you read. Note the shift in fonts that signals a shift in tone or intensity in your voice.

As I read I'd like you to:

- notice how Velvet is different from the group
- think about whether those are differences in how she looks, the way she acts, or something else
- notice how other characters react to the differences

- think about what the behaviors suggest about how those students feel about her differences
- think about what the behaviors of the other characters suggest about what those students believe about themselves.

AFTER THE READ ALOUD

Close the book and sit with the language for a few seconds. Resist the urge to tell your students what they are supposed to understand. Sit in silence and expect them to do the same. After ten to fifteen seconds, speak in a quiet voice.

- **Think on your own:** *Let's pause here and think about the meaning of this book. What does this text suggest for you?* Allow about forty seconds for this. [Think/Write]

  What do you understand from our work that Velvet's classmates didn't understand? How would you feel about Velvet if she were in our class?

  Think about the choices Velvet's classmates made. What choices would you make if you were in Velvet's class?

- **Stretch your thoughts with a partner:** *Now let's take about forty-five seconds to think together. Talk quietly with your partner, listen to your partner's ideas, share your thoughts, and think of a bumper sticker for this book.* [Share/Expand]

- **Share your new thinking:** *Let's share a few of your bumper stickers.* [Collaborate/Synthesize]

DAYS 2–3: EXTEND THIS THINKING UNTIL THE NEXT BOOK

Recall the insights from Layer 1 and Layer 2. Revisit the bumper stickers from those books and have students think about Velvet and her classmates. Here are a few things to think and write about over the next few days:

- *What do we understand about differences?*
- *What do we understand about people who are unkind to others who are different?*
- *In this book, Velvet didn't change, but her classmates did. Think about how that happened. Is there a bumper sticker for our brains?*
- *Think about any situation where getting to know someone has helped you change your thinking about a person and your behavior toward that person.*
- *What will you try to do differently now that we have shared this experience?*

LAYER 3: BOOK 5 (*CAMP K-9*)

Title: *Camp K-9*

Author: Mary Ann Rodman

Illustrator: Nancy Hayashi

2011 Peachtree ISBN 978–1–56145–561–4

Roxie, a cute little pooch, is headed to Camp K-9 along with a bus filled with other pups. She's a bit nervous because she has her blankie tucked away in her pooch pouch. She's never slept without it and she fears ridicule and teasing if the other campers discover her secret. On the bus she encounters a pushy poodle named Lacy who turns out to be something of a bully. But, as it turns out, Lacy has a secret, too.

DAY 1: INTRODUCE THE BOOK

VISUAL TOUR/READING THE ART

As we view the art I'd like you to:

- notice the eyes of the two characters on the cover
- notice that on the title page the main character (Roxie) has her belongings and appears to be going to camp (Look closely at her face. What does that expression suggest?)
- notice as you move through the art that Roxie's expressions change and think about why this is happening and how she is feeling
- notice the large white poodle (Lacy) and observe her behaviors
- notice the posture and expressions of the other characters
- notice the interactions among the characters
- notice details that let us know how others feel about Lacy's behavior
- notice when the posture and expressions of others begin to change
- think about what causes those changes to occur.

READ ALOUD

Read the book aloud with careful attention to pacing, tone, intensity, and mood. Note that our narrator is not homesick, but needs her blankie with her. That secret hovers over her and alters her perceptions of others. Note that Lacy presents a self-assured front to hide her own insecurity. Let your voice reflect the churning emotions in this book.

As I read I'd like you to:

- notice what Roxie fears most about being at camp
- think about details in the language that let us know
- think about how her fear influences her interactions
- notice how Lacy behaves, then think about why she keeps her pooch pouch with her all the time
- notice Lacy's behavior and how she reacts when she causes a problem for others
- notice how others react to Lacy's behavior
- notice what changes to make the other characters change
- think about how the group moves from distrust to trust and how new friendships are formed
- think about what the change in their behavior suggests about what they think and believe.

AFTER THE READ ALOUD

Close the book and sit with the language for a few seconds. Resist the urge to tell your students what they are supposed to understand. Sit in silence and expect them to do the same. After ten to fifteen seconds, speak in a quiet voice.

- **Think on your own:** *Let's pause here and think about the meaning of this book. What does this text suggest for you?* Allow about forty seconds for this. [Think/Write]

  Do we sometimes make up our minds about a person before we even get to know them? How did that happen in this story?

- **Stretch your thoughts with a partner:** *Now let's take about forty-five seconds to think together. Talk quietly with your partner, listen to your partner's ideas, share your thoughts, and think of a bumper sticker for this book.* [Share/Expand]

- **Share your new thinking:** *Let's share a few of your bumper stickers.* [Collaborate/Synthesize]

DAYS 2–3: EXTEND THIS THINKING UNTIL THE NEXT BOOK

Recall the insights from Layer 1 and Layer 2 and the thoughts from the books in this layer. Revisit the bumper stickers from those books and have students think about Roxie and her companions at Camp K-9. Here are a few things to think and write about over the next few days:

- *What do we understand now that we didn't before reading the book?*

- *In this book, both Roxie and Lacy were acting differently after the secret was out. And Roxie's thoughts about Lacy were very different after that. Think about why that happened. Is there a bumper sticker for our brains?*

- *Has there ever been a situation where getting to know someone has helped you change your thinking about a person and your behavior toward that person?*

- *The characters in this story are dogs — canines. Even though each of them is a different type of dog (collie, beagle, poodle, pug, etc.), all of them are dogs. How is this like what we have learned about people?*

- *Write about the insights we have gained from these first three layers. Can you put all those ideas into one bumper sticker? Can you make a list of attitudes and behaviors you want to work toward? What ideas, attitudes, and behaviors have you seen in any characters that you would like to change?*

- *How has this work changed the way you think and act with your classmates?*

- *What will you try to do differently now that we have shared this experience?*

CHAPTER 5

At the Core

When Others Are Not Thoughtful, Caring, and Kind

I've learned that people will forget what you said, people will forget what you did, but people will never forget how you made them feel.

—*Maya Angelou*

It has always been a mystery to me how men can feel themselves honoured by the humiliation of their fellow beings.

—*Mohandas Gandhi*

Working Through Layer 4

The focus of Layer 4 shifts to taking a deeper look into the behaviors of those who are unkind to others. In this inner layer we will examine a set of books in which characters blatantly bully others. These stories position us to examine bullying behaviors and bullying situations through the growing insights developed in the first three layers, so you may find it helpful to briefly review the essential understandings developed up to this point. Here, in Layer 4, we will examine the actions of the character exhibiting bullying behavior and consider alternative behaviors and choices. We will explore the notion that characters who exhibit bullying behaviors are not "bullies for life." We want to examine the situations in the text and work to determine whether there are circumstances that have left the character believing unkind behaviors are appropriate. Or if there is a set of beliefs being held by the bullying character that result in that behavior. We will explore the thoughts and feelings of characters portrayed as bullies, bullied, or bystanders. In addition, we examine the situations in which these events occur and use our insights and understandings from the first three layers as we consider what we could do if we find ourselves, or others, in similar situations. And at the end of each book we want to pause and reflect on what we can learn from the characters we have come to know.

Layer 4 in Action: Day 1

Lester worked with a group of second-grade students using Amanda Harvey's *Dog Eared*.

Opening Conversation

Lester: Good morning guys. It is good to be here with you again. Since I was here last I know you have read a few more books. The last book you read was *The Bully Blockers Club* by Teresa Bateman. Think for a moment about that book, remember the conversations you had and the thoughts you wrote in your notebooks. Let's just sit with those thoughts for a few seconds. [I pause for about forty seconds as most of the students sit in silence.]

Thank you. Turn to your partner and share your thinking. [I pause again allowing about forty to sixty seconds for the exchange.] Thanks, let's remember to use our mouths and our manners and hear from a few of you. Someone begin and tell us what your partner was thinking.

Second Grade: Ours was the same, we both said the same; treat others the way you want to be treated. Don't bully other people. Be nice to your friends. Speak up. Tell the teacher. Don't be a bully. Don't fight back just say "Stop it." Stand up for yourself and others. Speak up and watch out for each other. Bullies don't act like that when teachers are watching, that's why you need to have a club.

Lester: You did a lot of thinking about that book. So let's think about what it means for us. How does knowing this help us here at school?

Second Grade: If I see someone being a bully I'll say "Stop it," that's not kind. We will watch out for other kids on the playground and say, "Don't be a bully" if we see anybody being mean. I would go get a teacher so the teacher could fix it.

Read Aloud

Lester: I think we are ready for a new book titled *Dog Eared*. It is written and illustrated by Amanda Harvey. The main character is this dog on the cover of the book. His name is Otis and he is our narrator. We are going to read it all the way through without stopping. Then we are going to return to one page, look closely at the art, and do a lot of thinking. So your job now is to listen carefully and be thinking about the big messages here. Here we go. [I read the book aloud in a rather dramatic manner then close the book.]

After the Read Aloud

Lester: Stop and think for a minute. Let's think of a bumper sticker for this book. Remember, readers and writers are people who think. Sit with the ideas here for a moment. [We sit in silence for about forty seconds.] Now tell your bumper sticker to your neighbor.

Second Grade: Even if your body is different you are still like everybody else.

Lester: Oh, even if your body is different you are still like everybody else. Hmm, what made Otis' body different?

Second Grade: He had big ears. Yeah, his ears were really bigger.

Lester: He had longer ears. So even if your body is different you are still like everybody else. That's like the first book we read isn't it?

Second Grade: Yeah, even if we are different on the outside we are all the same on the inside.

Lester: And that is one of the big ideas in this book also. Let's hear a few more.

Second Grade: Treat everybody the way you want to be treated . . . even if they don't look like you. I said it doesn't matter what the bully says, you know in your heart what you really do. And I was thinking it is kind of like Bully Blockers Club . . . doesn't matter what you act, feel, and look like, you are still the same on the inside . . . I said if someone says something you don't have to worry about it all day . . . . You can't judge a dog by its outsides.

Lester: Oh, like you can't judge a book by its cover?

Second Grade: Yeah.

Lester: What if we said, "You can't judge a dog by its ears"? Let's try that with people instead of dogs. What would your bumper sticker say if we were talking about people?

Second Grade: You can't judge a person by their face . . . their looks . . . their skin color . . . .

Lester: That's just like our very first book, *Whoever You Are*, remember?

Second Grade: Yeah, it's like the same. Even though we are different on the outside, we are all the same inside.

Visual Tour/Reading the Art

Lester: Remember that I said we would come back to one picture and do some big thinking? I want us to look closely at this page. Notice the two dogs on this page. Notice how they are alike and how they are different. Remember the dog that was being a bully? Let's zoom in our attention on him. Notice his color is sort of a shade of yellow. Some people use the color yellow to say that a character is a coward. What's a coward?

Second Grade: When someone is trying to act big.

Lester: Yes, and coward is when someone is afraid to try things or to face challenges. The opposite of that would be courageous. Let's take a look at this art and think about what the bully dog might be afraid of. What was the first mean thing the yellow dog said to Otis?

Second Grade: "Out of my way, Big Ears."

Lester: Interesting . . . . Look at the ears on that yellow dog and tell me what you notice.

Second Grade: Oh my gosh! They are tiny! Yeah, his ears are really little . . . almost no ears at all. He's probably just wanting his ears to be big. He is jealous. He looks kind of like a bulldog, and it has bull in the beginning, and if you [makes a motion like stretching a rubber band] it is like bully . . . bully dog. Get it?

Lester: Oh yeah, he is a bully dog. I get it. Interesting observation. I hadn't noticed that. Now let's remember the second mean thing the yellow dog said to Otis.

Second Grade: He said "Outta my way, fat face."

Lester: Let's zoom in here; take a look at their faces. Which dog seems to have a flat or "fat" face?

Second Grade: The bully dog's face is scrunched in . . . Otis has a regular face . . . Wait! The bully dog is jealous of Otis and wants his face to be regular. He wants a long face.

Lester: Now look at the two dogs and think about what might happen if they were to meet in the park tomorrow. First he said, "Out of my way, Big Ears." Then he said "Out of my way, fat face." What do you think he would say next?

Second Grade: It's his tail. Otis has a long tail and the bully just about doesn't have a tail.

Lester: So what would he say?

Second Grade: "Out of my way, Long Tail"?

Lester: Interesting. What would he say if they met on the day after that?

Second Grade: Long legs . . . um . . . no wait . . . Otis has spots. He would say, "Out of my way, Spotty." And on the next day he might growl, "Out of my way, Long Fur."

Lester: He growls, perhaps he is feeling like Otis has something he wishes for. Or perhaps he is mean because he thinks these differences make Otis less important. Isn't it interesting that they are so different? How are they alike? Think back to our first book.

Second Grade: They are both dogs. They both have fur. They are both boys probably. They both have four legs and tails . . . .

Lester: Oh my, they are alike in so many, many ways. I want you to stop and think about something. Bumper sticker time! [One kid makes a three descending note tone . . . duh, da, daa.] Think. Sit with all these ideas and think about a bumper sticker. [I allow forty seconds.] Share your thinking with your partner. [I allow forty seconds.] Let's hear from you.

Second Grade: Treat others the way you want to be treated. Be nice to everyone. Just because you are different doesn't mean you don't have similarities to other people. We can be different but you are still the same and you can still be friends and have fun. All these books show that you are the same on the inside.

Lester: Should this make a difference in how we treat each other?

Second Grade: Yes! Don't bully. Pay attention to what people can do, not what they can't do. Bullies pay attention to what people can't do.

Lester: We have done a lot of work with this book today. While I am away, I'd like you to do some thinking in your notebook. Here's what I'd like you to think about: What big ideas show up in every book over and over? And I'd like you to think about what these messages mean . . . can people who are behaving like bullies change?

Essential Understandings for All Books in Layer 4:

- People who do not think of all others as fellow human beings can learn to appreciate difference.
- People who do not see others equally worthy of dignity and compassion can come to understand the power of kindness.
- People who think differences make one person more worthy or more important than another person can learn that no one is more important than another.
- People who are unkind or intentionally harmful to another human being can learn to change their beliefs and their behaviors.

LAYER 4: BOOK 1 (*BOOTSIE BARKER BITES*)

Title: *Bootsie Barker Bites*

Author: Barbara Bottner

Illustrator: Peggy Rathmann

1992 Putnam's Sons ISBN 0–399–22125–5

The young narrator in this story has a problem. Her mom and Bootsie's mom are best friends and they visit every day. The problem arises in the form of Bootsie's bossy, aggressive attitude. When our narrator talks with her mom about Bootsie's behavior she is told that she needs to learn to get along with all kinds of people. The situation reaches a peak when Bootsie is scheduled to spend the weekend at the narrator's house while her parents leave town for a trip to Chicago. Everyone learns some important lessons by the time we reach the last page.

DAY 1: INTRODUCE THE BOOK

VISUAL TOUR/READING THE ART

As we view the art I'd like you to:

- notice the two main characters and contrast the way they are presented (Name what you notice and give details from the art to support your thinking.)
- look closely at the facial expressions and posturing (What do these details suggest?)
- notice the actions of Bootsie (What do these actions suggest about what she thinks of the other girl?)
- notice the expressions and behaviors of our narrator. (What do these details suggest about what she is thinking?)

READ ALOUD

Read the book aloud with careful attention to pacing, tone, intensity, and mood. One character in this book seems to have a note of sarcasm and disdain in her voice. Let that be heard as you read. Note the emotions and thoughts of the narrator; let that come through your voice as you read.

As I read I'd like you to listen for:

- the way Bootsie speaks and what she has to say
- what the narrator says and thinks.

As I read I'd like you to think about:

- what Bootsie's words and tone reveal about her
- how Bootsie feels
- how our narrator is feeling
- the suggestion our narrator's mom makes (Does that seem like good advice for dealing with a bully? What would you suggest to her?)

AFTER THE READ ALOUD

Close the book and sit with the language for a few seconds. Resist the urge to tell your students what they are supposed to understand. Sit in silence and expect them to do the same. After ten to fifteen seconds, speak in a quiet voice.

- **Think on your own:** *Let's pause here and think about the meaning of this book. What does this text suggest for you?* Allow about forty seconds for this. [Think/Write]

  Think for a moment about why Bootsie talks and acts that way.

  Return to a page where Bootsie's behavior is unkind. Think about why that is happening. If you were playing with these two kids what could you do to help?

- **Stretch your thoughts with a partner:** *Now let's take about forty-five seconds to think together. Talk quietly with your partner, listen to your partner's ideas, share your thoughts, and think of a bumper sticker for this book.* [Share/Expand]

- **Share your new thinking:** *Let's share a few of your bumper stickers.* [Collaborate/Synthesize]

DAYS 2–3: EXTEND THIS THINKING UNTIL THE NEXT BOOK

Recall the insights from Layers 1, 2, and 3. Revisit the bumper stickers from those books. Here are a few things to think and write about over the next few days:

- *What do we understand from layers 1, 2, and 3 that can help us think about this book?*
- *In this book Bootsie is a bully. What could make her behave this way?*
- *Think about how Bootsie treats her playmate and think about what we know from our study. Since there were no bystanders, what could the narrator do to stop Bootsie?*

- *What have we learned that we could share with Bootsie? Or with our narrator?*
- *What can we learn from our narrator?*
- *Is there a bumper sticker in this for our brains?*
- *Write your thoughts about how we should respond if anyone is bullying us and no one else is around. What should we do? How can we avoid those situations?*
- *Create a role-playing situation where one child is Bootsie and the other child is being bullied.*
- *What will you try to do differently now that we have shared this experience?*

LAYER 4: BOOK 2 (*DOG EARED*)

Title: *Dog Eared*

Author: Amanda Harvey

Illustrator: Amanda Harvey

2002 Doubleday ISBN 0–385–72911–1

"'Out of my way, Big Ears!' Otis is happily strolling in the park one day when a bully dog taunts him with this insult. Poor Otis is crushed. Defeated! Suddenly his ears seem much too large. And he doesn't know what to do about them . . . . " [from the publisher]

DAY 1: INTRODUCE THE BOOK

VISUAL TOUR/READING THE ART

As we view the art I'd like you to:

- notice the dog on the front cover (His name is Otis and he is the narrator who is telling this story.)
- notice how pleasant and happy Otis looks on the cover and here on the title page
- notice how his posture, his ears, his tail, and his face change as we move through the art
- think about what could cause that change
- notice the other big dog here on the second page
- notice his color (a yellowish tone), his collar and leash, his face

- think about that yellow dog's attitude and what he may be feeling or thinking
- notice all the different ways Otis changes his ears as you move through the art
- look closely at the art and see where he is getting ideas for those changes
- think about why he is trying to change his ears
- notice on the last pages Otis seems happy and confident again
- think about what has given him that confidence.

READ ALOUD

Read the book aloud with careful attention to pacing, tone, intensity, and mood. There are two main voices in this book. One is the voice of our narrator, Otis. He is recounting a traumatic event; let your voice reflect that. The other voice is that of the bully, the yellow dog. He is gruff and growls at Otis. His voice should be intimidating. Let that be heard as you read.

As I read I'd like you to listen for:
- what happens to change the way Otis was feeling
- the different ways Otis tries to change his ears.

As I read I'd like you to think about:
- what the yellow dog said, the tone he used, and how that made Otis feel
- the way that yellow dog speaks to Otis
- why he speaks this way
- why Otis feels he needs to make his ears different
- why the yellow dog is saying mean things to Otis
- what the yellow dog may be saying to other dogs in the park.

AFTER THE READ ALOUD

Close the book and sit with the language for a few seconds. Resist the urge to tell your students what they are supposed to understand. Sit in silence and expect them to do the same. After ten to fifteen seconds, speak in a quiet voice.

- **Think on your own:** *Let's pause here and think about the meaning of this book. What does this text suggest for you?* Allow about forty seconds for this. [Think/Write]

  Think for a moment about the mean things the yellow dog said to Otis.

Now let's return to this page (the second and third pages). Look closely and compare the two dogs. Make notes about how they are alike and how they are different.

Recall the insult from the yellow dog — "Out of my way, Big Ears!" Compare the ears of the yellow dog and the ears of Otis. Think about why the yellow dog called Otis "Big Ears"

Think about what might have happened on the next day. If Otis met the yellow dog in the park what insult would he say next? And then, on the next day? And the next?

- **Stretch your thoughts with a partner:** *Now let's take about forty-five seconds to think together. Talk quietly with your partner, listen to your partner's ideas, share your thoughts, and think of a bumper sticker for this book.* [Share/Expand]

- **Share your new thinking:** *Let's share a few of your bumper stickers.* [Collaborate/Synthesize]

DAYS 2–3: EXTEND THIS THINKING UNTIL THE NEXT BOOK

Recall the insights from Layers 1, 2, and 3. Revisit the bumper stickers from those books and then think about Otis and the yellow dog. Here are a few things to think and write about over the next few days:

- *What do we understand now that can help us think about this book?*

- *In this book, Otis felt fine until the yellow dog said something mean. He tried very hard to make himself different. Then he felt better when Lucy said she loved his ears. What important lesson does Otis still need to learn?*

- *What have we learned that we could share with Otis?*

- *In this book the yellow dog said mean things to Otis. We noticed that the yellow dog's insults reflect his own features (his small ears, his pug face). Is there a bumper sticker in this for our brains?*

- *What have we learned that we could share with the yellow dog?*

- *In this book we gave a lot of thought to the reasons the yellow dog was growling unkind remarks to Otis. We agreed he could feel that he was not as good and was jealous of Otis. Or perhaps he believed that he was perfect and anyone different was not as good as him. Write about how this book can help us think about how we can respond to others who behave like bullies. Can we help people who behave like bullies change their behavior and become friends?*

- *What will you try to do differently now that we have shared this experience?*

LAYER 4: BOOK 3 (*THE RECESS QUEEN*)

Title: *The Recess Queen*

Author: Alexis O'Neill

Illustrator: Laura Huliska-Beith

2002 Scholastic ISBN 0–439–20637–3

Jean is a playground bully who rules the schoolyard. No one dares stand up to her and no one ever invites her to join in their play. But everything changes when a new kid, the tiny Katie Sue, comes to school. Katie Sue doesn't know the "rules" or the "rep" of the Recess Queen and jumps right in to play. When Jean blows a fuse, Katie Sue is non-plussed and invites Jean to join her in jumping rope. The dynamics quickly change on the playground after that.

DAY 1: INTRODUCE THE BOOK

VISUAL TOUR/READING THE ART

As we view the art I'd like you to:

- Notice Jean front and center on the cover. Quickly note her posture, the clinched fists, the menacing look on her face, and that crown she is wearing.
- Notice the five other children scattering off the page. Note the look on each of their faces and the way they scurry to get out of her path.
- Think about what this image suggests.
- Notice how Jean is portrayed as more powerful, more aggressive, and unflinching on each spread.
- Notice that Jean is almost always playing alone.
- Notice the small details around the other characters and think about what these suggest.
- Notice the size of the new kid, Katie Sue, who shows up in the middle of the story.
- Examine the expressions of all the other characters when the new kid arrives; look closely at Jean and think about what she is planning.
- Notice the freedom and joy in Katie Sue's face and actions when she bursts onto the playground. Notice how the perspective shifts at this point. Think about what that is suggesting.

- Contrast that image with the image of Jean moving across the playground toward Katie Sue.
- Examine the close up of the meeting of Katie Sue and Jean. Think about what the details reveal here.
- Continue to examine each subsequent spread contrasting the expressions and actions of each girl. Notice what other characters are doing in the background.
- When Jean's expression changes, think about what has caused that to occur.
- Pause and linger with the images on the final spread and the closing page. Notice the changes and think about what has happened.

READ ALOUD

Read the book aloud with careful attention to pacing, tone, intensity, and mood. Jean seems to have a note of arrogance and aggression in her voice. Let that be heard as you read. Note the shift in fonts that signals a shift in tone or intensity in your voice.

As I read I'd like you to listen for:
- the words used to describe Jean and how she acts
- what she has done to become known as "Mean Jean the Recess Queen"
- the words used to describe how she treats others
- the description of the new kid, Katie Sue.

As I read I'd like you to think about:
- how the other characters would feel about Jean
- whether Jean is the kind of person who gets invited to play after school, or to come to birthday parties, or to a sleepover
- Jean, who almost always plays alone (Do you think she prefers to be alone with no friends? Think about why she would act this way.)
- the words used to describe how Katie Sue acts on the playground
- the language used to describe the confrontation between Jean and Katie Sue
- how you would feel if a bigger kid did that to you or someone you know on your first day in a new school
- how Katie Sue reacts to Jean's aggressive and bossy ways
- how Katie Sue uses her words and actions to change the situation.

AFTER THE READ ALOUD

Close the book and sit with the language for a few seconds. Resist the urge to tell your students what they are supposed to understand. Sit in silence and expect them to do the same. After ten to fifteen seconds, speak in a quiet voice.

- **Think on your own:** *Let's pause here and think about the meaning of this book. What does this text suggest for you?* Allow about forty seconds for this. [Think/Write]

  Think for a moment about the way Jean treats others and speaks to them. Who are her friends? What does she seem to think of others?

  Now let's return to the page where Jean confronts Katie Sue on the playground. Think about Jean's actions and her words. Think about why she may be acting this way.

  Is there any evidence that Jean wants to have friends? What do you think about that?

  Think about this: "Mean Jean Recess Queen" is part of her identity. That is how she is known. So how does that make everyone treat her?

  Think about this: If everyone treats her like she is a bully and no one treats her like a friend then how do we expect her to act?

  Think about this: The new kid doesn't know anything about anyone in the class. What does that make you think about?

- **Stretch your thoughts with a partner:** *Now let's take about forty-five seconds to think together. Talk quietly with your partner, listen to your partner's ideas, share your thoughts, and think of a bumper sticker for this book.* [Share/Expand]

- **Share your new thinking:** *Let's share a few of your bumper stickers.* [Collaborate/Synthesize]

DAYS 2–3: EXTEND THIS THINKING UNTIL THE NEXT BOOK

Recall the insights from Layers 1, 2, and 3. Revisit the bumper stickers from those books. Here are a few things to think and write about over the next few days:

- *What do we understand now that can help us think about this book?*

- *In this book, Jean lived up to her reputation. Everyone expected her to act a certain way and she did. What if everyone began to think of her in a different way? What if her classmates began to treat her like a friend like Katie Sue did? What if everyone began to expect something different?*

- *What have we learned that we could share with Jean?*
- *What can we learn from Katie Sue? What does she know that we have learned from thinking about other books?*
- *Is there a bumper sticker in this for our brains?*
- *What will you try to do differently now that we have shared this experience?*

LAYER 4: BOOK 4 (*THE BULLY BLOCKERS CLUB*)

Title: *The Bully Blockers Club*

Author: Teresa Bateman

Illustrator: Jackie Urbanovic

2004 Albert Whitman ISBN 978–0–8075–0919–7

"Lotty Raccoon is very excited about her first day of school, until she has to sit next to Grant Grizzly. He kicks her desk, steals her lunch, and calls her names. She tries to ignore him, then tries to make friends with him, but nothing seems to make this bully go away . . . . But Lotty's not the only one Grant picks on. And soon, Lotty and her classmates form the Bully Blockers Club—by standing together, they won't be bullied anymore." [from the publisher]

DAY 1: INTRODUCE THE BOOK

VISUAL TOUR/READING THE ART

As we view the art I'd like you to:
- notice the expression on Lotty's face as she is leaving for the first day of school
- notice the new class on the second page (Look closely at the expressions and posture of the characters. Can you tell which character will be the bully? Target?)
- think about what Lotty is doing and thinking when she is at home
- notice the faces and body language of all the characters when Grant is unkind to anyone
- think about how Lotty brings a solution to the situation.

READ ALOUD

Read the book aloud with careful attention to pacing, tone, intensity, and mood. Read the text a couple of times before reading it aloud to your class. You'll want to make sure your voice reflects the shifting emotions of Lotty and the arrogant stance of Grant, which softens near the conclusion.

As I read I'd like you to listen for:

* the behavior of the other characters when Grant is being unkind (Why are they behaving this way? What are they thinking? How does this make Grant feel?)
* the words Grant uses to make others fear him
* Grant's words and actions. (What do these tell us about him? Can we venture a guess about why he is unkind to others?)

As I read I'd like you to think about:

* why Lotty is reluctant to tell her teacher or her parents (What does she fear?)
* what Lotty does to try and cope with Grant's unkind behavior (How is she feeling?)
* why other classmates don't speak up or help Lotty
* what Grant says when he is called up to the teacher with Lotty (What does he say? Why doesn't Lotty speak up?)
* Grant's behavior with others (Why doesn't anyone tell an adult? Or step up to help? Why is everyone being a bystander?)
* how Lotty solves the problem. (What does that suggest for us?)

AFTER THE READ ALOUD

Close the book and sit with the language for a few seconds. Resist the urge to tell your students what they are supposed to understand. Sit in silence and expect them to do the same. After ten to fifteen seconds, speak in a quiet voice.

* **Think on your own:** *Let's pause here and think about the meaning of this book. What does this text suggest for you?* Allow about forty seconds for this. [Think/Write]

   Think for a moment about Grant's unkind comments and behaviors.

   Think about how Lotty felt for days and days.

Think about how the advice Lotty got from family and friends becomes part of her plan for a Bully Blockers Club.

- **Stretch your thoughts with a partner:** *Now let's take about forty-five seconds to think together. Talk quietly with your partner, listen to your partner's ideas, share your thoughts, and think of a bumper sticker for this book.* [Share/Expand]

- **Share your new thinking:** *Let's share a few of your bumper stickers.* [Collaborate/Synthesize]

DAYS 2–3: EXTEND THIS THINKING UNTIL THE NEXT BOOK

Option 1: Recall the insights from Layers 1, 2, and 3. Revisit the bumper stickers from those books, and then have students think about Grant's words and actions. Think also about Lotty. Here are some things to think and write about over the next few days.

- *What do we understand now that can help us think about this book?*

- *In this book, Grant was being unkind with his words and his behavior. What does that tell us about what he thinks is important?*

- *Think about all we have learned. Think about how this book ends. Do you have thoughts that may explain why Grant was behaving like a bully for a while?*

- *Think about this. In the beginning of the story Grant behaves like a bully. And by the end of the story Grant's actions are kind and helpful. What does this change show us? What does that make you think about?*

- *What have we learned that we could share with Lotty? Or with Grant?*

- *What have we learned so far that we could have done if this had happened in our class?*

Option 2: Revisit the suggestions Lotty and her class came up with. Return to the scene where the teacher has written their suggestions on the board. Review the list and invite the children to talk about why "fight back" has been crossed off.

Option 3: Turn to the last page and share the suggestions there regarding the "tell it" system.

Option 4: By now students have worked through several books, thought about many situations, and come up with several bumper stickers for insights and ideas across the layers. Have students turn to a clean page in their notebook and write about how they are different because of what they now know.

LAYER 4: BOOK 5 (*BULLY*)

Title: *Bully*

Author: Judith Caseley

Illustrator: Judith Caseley

2001 harperchildren ISBN 1–688–17867–7

"Jack . . . was a bully. And he made life very uncomfortable for Mickey . . . Mickey's parents had some helpful ideas, but Mickey found that it was easier to talk about loving your enemies than actually doing it, and brave words were often just words. But then something happened that surprised Mickey as much as Jack. And the unexpected result was that the ex-bully was once more a friend, and Mickey had good reason to be proud of his problem-solving technique." [from the publisher]

DAY 1: INTRODUCE THE BOOK

VISUAL TOUR/READING THE ART

As we view the art I'd like you to:

- look closely at the first few scenes (It seems like a typical playground and everyone is getting along well.)
- notice the two boys climbing the monkey bars on the third page (Look closely and think about what is happening there.)
- notice on the fourth page as the two boys, Mickey and Jack, face off (What does this posture and expression suggest?)
- watch those two characters in the next several pages (Notice the changes in expressions, notice their actions, and think about what these changes suggest.)
- on the page where Jack is smiling with his new braces, look closely and think about what is different about Jack
- on the next page something is shifting (Notice the expressions and gestures of the group. Notice the change in Jack's posture. Notice Mickey's face and think about what has happened and what the boys are thinking and feeling.)
- notice the big change in the next three scenes. (What do these changes in expression and behavior now suggest?)

READ ALOUD

Read the book aloud with careful attention to pacing, tone, intensity, and mood. Read through the text a couple of times to find a rhythm that works. Note there will be emotions present in the voices of both Mickey and Jack. Those emotions shift as the story develops; be sure to reflect that in the tone of your read aloud voice.

As I read I'd like you to:

- notice the way Jack's attitude and actions quickly change in the first two pages (Think about the reason(s) for the change in his attitude and his behavior.)
- think about all you know about bullies (Do you think Jack has always been a bully? Will he always be a bully? Can a person become a bully and then stop being a bully?)
- think about why Jack picks on Mickey
- think about what the other kids in the class do when Jack is being unkind
- notice Mickey's actions and think about what is happening
- think about the advice Mickey gets from his parents (What else could we suggest for him to try?)
- think about what Mickey understood about Jack. (How did that understanding make a difference?)

AFTER THE READ ALOUD

Close the book and sit with the language for a few seconds. Resist the urge to tell your students what they are supposed to understand. Sit in silence and expect them to do the same. After ten to fifteen seconds, speak in a quiet voice.

- **Think on your own:** *Let's pause here and think about the meaning of this book. What does this text suggest for you?* Allow about forty seconds for this. [Think/Write]

  Think for a moment about why Jack switched from friend to bully. Then from bully to friend.

  Now let's return to the page where the class is laughing at Jack and calling him "track-mouth Jack." Think for a moment about what Jack is feeling. What might he be thinking? Do you have any evidence from the story for your ideas?

  What is Mickey thinking and feeling while this is happening to Jack? Do you have any evidence from the story to support your ideas?

- **Stretch your thoughts with a partner:** *Now let's take about forty-five seconds to think together. Talk quietly with your partner, listen to your partner's ideas, share your thoughts, and think of a bumper sticker for this book.* [Share/Expand]

- **Share your new thinking:** *Let's share a few of your bumper stickers.* [Collaborate/Synthesize]

DAYS 2–3: EXTEND THIS THINKING UNTIL THE NEXT BOOK

Recall the insights from Layers 1, 2, and 3. Revisit the bumper stickers from those books. In the next few days have students think and write about:

- *What do we understand now that can help us think about this book?*

- *In this book Jack becomes a bully. We noticed that he wasn't always a bully. Think about how that happened and think about what we know from our study. Recall Grant's behavior in the Bully Blockers Club and remember how he began as a bully but ended up as a friend. If we think about these two stories together, what does that help us to understand about bully behaviors and bystander behaviors?*

- *What have we learned that we could share with Jack? Or with Mickey?*

- *What can we learn from Mickey?*

- *Is there a bumper sticker in this for our brains?*

- *Write your thoughts about what could make a person behave like a bully. As you are organizing your thoughts, consider how a person could behave like a bully for a while and then become a friend.*

- *Reflect on the bumper sticker from Layer 1 (we are more alike on the inside than we are different on the outside) or (we are different on the outside, but the same on the inside). If we believe that all the things that make us human are present in everyone else (even people who behave like bullies), then how do we find the good person behind the bully behavior?*

- *What will you try to do differently now that we have shared this experience?*

CHAPTER 6

Getting Focused for Action
An Opportunity to Explore the Actions of Others, Reflect on Our Own Feelings, and Redirect Our Behaviors Toward Fellow Human Beings

When I say it's you I like, I'm talking about that part of you that knows that life is far more than anything you can ever see or hear or touch. That deep part of you that allows you to stand for those things without which humankind cannot survive. Love that conquers hate, peace that rises triumphant over war, and justice that proves more powerful than greed.
                                    –Fred Rogers

It's not the comments of our enemies that matter, it's the silence of our friends.
                                    –Martin Luther King, Jr.

Working Through Layer 5

This final layer is the space where all the previous thinking becomes the lens through which we view the world around us. Throughout the read aloud experiences and the guided conversations you have worked together to develop a core of understanding that becomes the guiding principles for how we interact in a kind and compassionate community. These principles become the lens for how we view ourselves and others:

Essential Understandings
Layer 1:
◉ As human beings, we are more alike than different.
◉ Those things that make each of us human are present in every other human across the globe.
Level 2:
◉ Within the range of humanity, there are differences.
◉ Some differences are more obvious than others.
◉ The differences that exist within the range of humanity do not make any of us more human or less human.
◉ Any difference or combination of differences does not alter the fact that we are all human and does not take away any of the aspects we all share as members of the human family.
◉ A difference does not make another human better than others or less than others; a difference merely makes us different.
Level 3:
◉ Our actions reflect our beliefs and feelings, our thoughts and values.
◉ How we treat other people shows what we believe about ourselves and our relationship to other human beings.
◉ Unkind behavior toward another person shows a sense of feeling more important or less important than others.
Level 4:
◉ People who do not think of all others as fellow human beings can learn to appreciate difference.

- People who do not see others equally worthy of dignity and compassion can come to understand the power of kindness.
- People who think differences make one person more worthy or more important than another person can learn that no one is more important than another.
- People who are unkind or intentionally harmful to another human being can learn to change their beliefs and their behaviors.

Level 5:

- I am responsible for my thoughts and feelings.
- I am responsible for my actions.
- I am responsible for the way I treat others.
- I choose to be a bystander or a defender when others are being bullied.
- I am enough; I do not succumb to the attempts of others to build themselves up by making me feel intimidated or lessened.
- I am enough; I do not need to make others feel lessened in order to feel that I am enough.
- Making someone else feel bad does not make me feel better.
- Making someone else frightened does not make me feel powerful and important.
- I am part of the human family.
- Everything that makes me human is present in all other people.
- I respect myself and I think and act accordingly.

Through this lens we focus on the responsibilities that come with understanding and knowledge. Essentially we address these questions:

- How am I different now that I have this understanding?
- How does this understanding influence the way I think of others?
- How does this understanding influence the way I treat others?
- How does this understanding influence the way I respond when others are being mistreated?

The books we selected for Layer 5 offer examples of individuals who have these understandings in place and act on them in daily life. As you lead your students through each of these books keep in mind that at least one character has that inner strength and acts on the essential understandings for Layer 5. The read aloud experiences with these books offer your students the opportunity to identify those characters and the character traits each of them possess. Explore the thoughts, decisions, feelings, and actions of those characters. Lead your students toward putting their insights into action. Layer by layer your students have gained insight into their own humanity and their kinship to all other human beings. Layer by layer you have worked together to deepen a shared knowledge of the responsibility each of us has to respect others and ourselves. Layer 5 is where we bring all this together into forming both individual and community action plans.

Layer 5 in Action: Day 1

Lester worked with a group of fourth graders using Kathryn Otoshi's *One*.

Opening Conversation

Lester: Before we take a look at a new book I want you to think about the things you've been writing in your notebooks. We've been thinking about several books. Take a moment to think about what we have come to understand so far. Sit with that idea and think for a moment. [I allow forty-five seconds.] Quietly talk with your partner about your thoughts. [I allow forty-five seconds.] Let's hear what you and your partners have been thinking.

Fourth Grade: People are the same all over the world. We may have differences, like Ian in the book was autistic and Moses in the other book was deaf, but they are still people. Differences don't mean that you aren't still a person. Bullies like to target anyone who is different. A bully can be a good person; I mean a person who is being a bully is still a person like everyone else. They're just doing mean things. But they can learn to stop and be friends. If someone is being a bully we should tell that person to cut it out. And everyone should gather around the one being bullied and tell the bully to stop it.

Lester: Wow, you guys have been thinking. I hope these ideas are becoming part of how you think and act when you are with other children on the playground and around the school.

Read Aloud

Lester: Today I'm going to share a book I really, really like. This one is written and illustrated by Kathryn Otoshi. The title is *One*. This book is a little different. The characters are not people. And they are not animals. Instead the characters in this book are colors, just spots of color. I'm going to begin reading and I will read all the way through without stopping. At the end we will come back to any page you'd like and talk about what this book has helped us think about. [I read aloud with careful attention to tone so that the emotion of "characters" could be sensed. As I reach the end of the book I simply close the cover and sit for a few seconds before speaking.]

After the Read Aloud

Lester: Sit with the big ideas in this book. I invite you to think about the bullying behaviors of Red and the bystander behaviors of Yellow, Green, Purple, and Orange. I invite you to think about how Blue felt when no one spoke up, when no one helped. So let's sit with our thoughts about that for just a few seconds. [I allow forty seconds.] Share your thinking with your partner. [Short pause.] I can tell this one has sparked a lot of thoughts. Let's hear from a few of you.

Fourth Grade: Red got bigger and bigger every time he bullied Blue. Yeah, and when none of the other colors spoke up Red gained power. Red got so powerful he started to bully every color. And then it was too late for the other colors to help because they lost their power.

Lester: We have lots of thoughts about Red and his bullying behaviors. It's also interesting that you are thinking about who has power here. I'm wondering about Blue. What were your thoughts on how Blue was feeling and why Blue didn't speak up?

Fourth Grade: Blue felt good about being blue except when he was with Red. He felt blue—get it? When Red said red is hot, blue is not then Blue felt sad. We think Blue was sad because Red was mean, but also because his friends didn't do anything to help. I think all the colors felt blue when they lost their power and Red had all the power.

Lester: So when bullies take power, victims and bystanders lose power?

Fourth Grade: Yes. [Many signal their agreement.]

Lester: Think about how the power shifted when One came along. Think about how One's attitude was different and how his actions were different; think about how that changed everything. Let's sit with our thoughts a few seconds then we'll share with partners. [I allow forty seconds.] Share your thoughts and remember to listen as much as you speak [I allow forty to sixty seconds.] Let's hear your thinking.

Fourth Grade: When One came along he wasn't just like everyone else. He was tall, like he stood up, he counted. Yeah, he believed he mattered and that Red didn't have a right to act that way. And when one spoke up and said No, Red starting losing power. So the other colors felt braver and stronger. Yellow wanted to count, so he became a number and then the other colors did too. It's like the *Bully Blockers Club* that we read. Oh yeah, when everyone stands up the bully has no power. The colors became numbers and took all their power back.

Lester: So the colors learned something from One and they took back their power and Red lost power. Now I invite you to think about what happens to Red at the end of the book. Pause and remember how he changes and how that happened. [I allow forty seconds.] Share your thinking with your partner. [I allow forty to sixty seconds.] Let's hear your thinking now.

Fourth Grade: At the end Red was little again. He didn't have any more power than anyone else and he felt really small. I think Red felt embarrassed because no one was afraid of him anymore. Yeah, like he said, Red was embarrassed and was running away feeling bad.

Lester: So Red learned that when others stand up to him he doesn't have power. And that made him feel small and embarrassed, not so important. But something else happened. Think about this; when the other colors became numbers—when they stood up and counted and took back their power—they could have become the bullies and they could have ganged up on Red and bullied him. Think about all we have learned from our study of the books in all five layers. Think about One and the colors standing up together, counting, and claiming their power. Think about what they did, especially think about what Blue did at the end.

Fourth Grade: Oh, Blue said Red could count too. Blue asked if Red could be hot and Blue could be super cool . . . so both could be important. Blue was being kind when he could have been a bully, but he knew how it felt to be a victim. And all the other colors invited Red to count too.

Lester: Here we have a bully who became a friend. We have someone who was a victim who learned to stand up and speak up. We have friends who were bystanders that learned to stand together and speak up when someone is being unkind. And all that happened because only one person had the courage to use his power to stand up and say "No, stop it; that is not acceptable behavior." That's a powerful thought.

I'd like you to continue thinking about this book. In your notebooks, I'd like you to write about what this book causes you to think. I'd also like you to do two other things. First, think about and design a bumper sticker that could stand for all the ideas we have come up with; one big message that can stand for all the books in all the layers. And second, write your thoughts about what you can do to be like one.

Essential Understandings for All Books in Layer 5:

- I am responsible for my thoughts and feelings.
- I am responsible for my actions.
- I am responsible for the way I treat others.
- I choose to be a bystander or a defender when others are being bullied.
- I am enough; I do not succumb to the attempts of others to build themselves up by making me feel intimidated or lessened.
- I am enough; I do not need to make others feel lessened in order to feel that I am enough.
- Making someone else feel bad does not make me feel better.
- Making someone else frightened does not make me feel powerful and important.
- I am part of the human family.
- Everything that makes me human is present in all other people.
- I respect myself and I think and act accordingly.

LAYER 5: BOOK 1 (*STAND TALL, MOLLY LOU MELON*)

Title: *Stand Tall, Molly Lou Melon*

Author: Patty Lovell

Illustrator: David Catrow

2001 Putnam ISBN 0–399–23416–0

Molly Lou would be a bully's dream target. She's "just taller than her dog" with huge buck teeth and a croak of a voice. To top it off she's "often fumble fingered." But Molly Lou Melon has a grandmother who has infused her with a sense of worthiness and dignity that can't be toppled even when she enters a new school and meets a bully named Ronald Durkin.

DAY 1: INTRODUCE THE BOOK

VISUAL TOUR/READING THE ART

As we view the art I'd like you to:

- notice the exaggerated features of Molly Lou's physical appearance
- notice her size and stature in comparison to the things around her
- notice the expression on her face and the exuberance in her actions.

READ ALOUD

Read the book aloud with careful attention to pacing, tone, intensity, and mood. The narrator voice carries the story. The shift in tone and intensity comes when Ronald Durkin speaks. Let his sarcasm and aggression be heard in your voice.

As I read I'd like you to:
- notice how Molly Lou is described
- notice what her grandmother tells her
- notice how Molly Lou doesn't let anything keep her from enjoying life
- notice what happens when she is confronted by Ronald Durkin and think about how she reacts to his bullying.

AFTER THE READ ALOUD

Close the book and sit with the language for a few seconds. Resist the urge to tell your students what they are supposed to understand. Sit in silence and expect them to do the same. After ten to fifteen seconds, speak in a quiet voice.

- **Think on your own:** *Let's pause here and think about the meaning of this book. What does this text suggest for you?* Allow about forty seconds for this. [Think/Write]

  Think for a moment about all the ways Molly Lou is different.

  Think about all the ways she is like every other human on the globe.

  Consider the ways Ronald Durkin tried to make her feel less than others and think about why he acted that way.

  Recall what you know of Molly Lou. How did she become this self-assured?

- **Stretch your thoughts with a partner:** *Now let's take about forty-five seconds to think together. Talk quietly with your partner, listen to your partner's ideas, share your thoughts, and think of a bumper sticker for this book.* [Share/Expand]

- **Share your new thinking:** *Let's share a few of your bumper stickers.* [Collaborate/Synthesize]

DAYS 2–3: EXTEND THIS THINKING UNTIL THE NEXT BOOK

Recall the insights from Layers 1 through 4. Revisit the bumper stickers from those books. In the next few days, have students think and write about some of the following:

- *Think about the essential understandings we have charted as we studied each of the books so far. How do we see those understandings at work in this story?*

- *In this book Molly Lou is undaunted by the attempts of Ronald Durkin to make her feel unimportant and unworthy. Is there a bumper sticker in this for our brains?*

- *What have we learned from Molly Lou that we could do ourselves?*

- *Reflect on all the work we have done in Layers 1 through 4 and find examples that show how Molly Lou understands and lives those ideas.*

- *Write your thoughts about how you can be more like Molly. What examples can you include to show how your behaviors and words demonstrate what you now understand?*

- *What can we do as a classroom community to make kindness matter?*

- *What can we do in our classroom to show our respect for others and ourselves?*

- *What can we do to help each person in the classroom community have self-respect and respect for others?*

LAYER 5: BOOK 2 (*HEY LITTLE ANT*)

Title: *Hey Little Ant*

Authors: Phillip and Hannah Hoose

Illustrator: Debbie Tilley

1998 Tricycle Press ISBN 978–1883672546

A young boy spots an ant on the sidewalk and announces his intentions to squish the ant with his raised up shoe. The kid is urged by his peers to squish the ant. The ant pleads for mercy. The text is presented as a dialogue alternating between the ant and the kid with the ant attempting to convince the kid of what they have in common as living creatures. The book ends with a raised up shoe and the reader has to make the final decision.

DAY 1: INTRODUCE THE BOOK

VISUAL TOUR/READING THE ART

As we view the art I'd like you to:

- notice the contrast in size of the kid and the ant
- think about all we have learned about bullies and their behavior
- notice the kid could clearly overpower the ant
- think about what the ant is attempting
- think about what the kid is considering.

READ ALOUD

Read the book aloud with careful attention to pacing, tone, intensity, and mood. Notice the text is presented as a script alternating between the kid and the ant. Read the text aloud a couple of times to find the voice you feel is best suited to each character. Be attentive to the emotional tone in the voice of each character. Remember the ant is trying to convince this kid to spare his life.

As I read I'd like you to listen for:

- what the kid says to the ant and think about how his attitude and behavior is like that of a bully
- the voice of the ant and think about the essential understandings from earlier books.

As I read I'd like you to think about:

- which essential understandings the ant has the kid thinking about
- the bumper sticker we could write to remind us of this important insight.

AFTER THE READ ALOUD

Close the book and sit with the language for a few seconds. Resist the urge to tell your students what they are supposed to understand. Sit in silence and expect them to do the same. After ten to fifteen seconds, speak in a quiet voice.

- **Think on your own:** *Let's pause here and think about the meaning of this book. What does this text suggest for you?* Allow about forty seconds for this. [Think/Write]
  Think for a moment about what the ant is teaching the kid (and maybe us).
  Think about why the kid believes it is appropriate to squish ants.

Let's return to this page (where the ant is larger than the kid). What is the ant helping the kid think about? Look closely and think about other books we have examined. How could this experience have helped in other stories? What other stories have we read that could help in this situation?

- **Stretch your thoughts with a partner:** *Now let's take about forty-five seconds to think together. Talk quietly with your partner, listen to your partner's ideas, share your thoughts, and think of a bumper sticker for this book.* [Share/Expand]

- **Share your new thinking:** *Let's share a few of your bumper stickers.* [Collaborate/Synthesize]

DAYS 2–3: EXTEND THIS THINKING UNTIL THE NEXT BOOK

Recall the insights from Layers 1 through 4. Revisit the bumper stickers from those books. In the next few days, have students think and write about some of the following:

- *In this book the kid is much more powerful than the ant and believes the ant doesn't matter. Think about how this situation is similar to the situations in other books we have read.*

- *Now let's return to the last page where the ant is standing in the shadow of the kid's shoe. Consider all that we have come to understand through our study of bullying. What would you say to this kid?*

- *In this book the ant uses his words and appeals to the humanity of the kid. Is there a bumper sticker in this for our brains?*

- *The boy had much more power and is now in a position to use his judgment. The decision he makes will show us what he believes. Write your thoughts about power and judgment.*

- *Think about situations you have seen, read, or heard about where someone used power to help another person.*

- *What can we do as a classroom community to make kindness matter?*

- *What can we do in our classroom to show our respect for others and ourselves?*

- *What can we do to help each person in the classroom community have self-respect and respect for others?*

LAYER 5: BOOK 3 (*A CHANCE TO SHINE*)

Title: *A Chance to Shine*

Authors: Steve Seskin and Allen Shamblin

Illustrator: R. Gregory Christie

2006 Tricycle Press ISBN 978–1582461670

"Sometimes we just need a chance to show how great we can become. When Joe is given his chance to shine, one young boy's eyes are opened in a way that changes him forever. This tale of compassion sets a shining example of how a kind act by one can make a big difference to many." [from the publisher]

DAY 1: INTRODUCE THE BOOK

VISUAL TOUR/READING THE ART

As we view the art I'd like you to:

- think about which character could become a target of unkindness
- think about which character or characters may use knowledge, understanding, and kindness to help another character
- notice the man sitting on the bench surrounded by the pigeons (Use what you have learned as you think about his situation. What are your thoughts about who he is and why he is here?)
- notice the man with the broom raised over his head (Look closely at his face. Think about what he is feeling. Think about what he may be saying here.)
- notice the man from the park walking away (Think about why. What do you think the man with the broom is saying to the young boy?)
- notice the man sweeping (Think about what has happened here. Does this change your thinking from the pages before?)
- notice the expressions and interactions of the characters on the next several pages (Think about what has happened here.)
- notice the kid in the red shirt with the soccer ball in the scene moving from the storefront to a school playground (This is the kid from the sidewalk. Think about what he is doing. Notice the other kids in red shirts on the right side of the page. Look closely at them. Notice where their eyes

are looking; notice how they seem to be whispering. Think about what they are saying.)

- notice the change in expressions and posture on the next two pages. (Think about what has happened. Why has this happened?)

READ ALOUD

Read the book aloud with careful attention to pacing, tone, intensity, and mood. The narrator, the young boy, carries the story. The text is written in a rhyme pattern, but be careful to not let rhyme override the power of the language. Focus on the meaning. So read this aloud a couple of times before reading it to your students.

As I read I'd like you to listen for:

- how Joe, the guy on the bench, is described (Think about how he could become a target of unkind words and actions.)
- how the father's kindness is a reflection of what he believes about others
- how the boy (our narrator) comes to understand the power of his father's kindness.

As I read I'd like you to think about:

- how this story may have been different if the father held other beliefs about people who seem different
- how the father's actions are a reflection of what we have learned so far
- how the boy has changed by the time he goes back to school.

AFTER THE READ ALOUD

Close the book and sit with the language for a few seconds. Resist the urge to tell your students what they are supposed to understand. Sit in silence and expect them to do the same. After ten to fifteen seconds, speak in a quiet voice.

- **Think on your own:** *Let's pause here and think about the meaning of this book. What does this text suggest for you?* Allow about forty seconds for this. [Think/Write]

   Think for a moment of reasons Joe could have become a target.

   Think of examples of how Joe is like every other human on the globe.

   Think of examples of how the boy and his dad focused on Joe's common humanity.

   Recall how Joe was portrayed in the beginning and how he was portrayed in the end. How did that transformation occur?

- **Stretch your thoughts with a partner:** *Now let's take about forty-five seconds to think together. Talk quietly with your partner, listen to your partner's ideas, share your thoughts, and think of a bumper sticker for this book.* [Share/Expand]
- **Share your new thinking:** *Let's share a few of your bumper stickers.* [Collaborate/Synthesize]

DAYS 2–3: EXTEND THIS THINKING UNTIL THE NEXT BOOK

Recall the insights from Layers 1 through 4. Revisit the bumper stickers from those books. In the next few days have students think and write about some of the following:

- *Think about the essential understandings we have charted as we studied each of the books so far. How do we see those understandings at work in this story?*
- *In this book Joe is someone who may have been harassed by others. Instead he is helped by the kindness of others and it makes a difference. Who is changed by this kindness? Is there a bumper sticker in this for our brains?*
- *What have we learned from Joe, the boy, and his dad that we could do ourselves?*
- *In this story Joe was a person with very few resources and very little power. The boy and his dad had the power and resources to run Joe out of the park. Instead, they offered him a way to keep his dignity, get food, earn some money, and get his power back. What does this show us about the thoughts and beliefs of the boy's dad? How is that like the thoughts and beliefs of Molly Lou Melon?*
- *If you shared those same thoughts and beliefs what would have to change in the way you behave and treat others?*
- *What can we do as a classroom community to make kindness matter?*
- *What can we do in our classroom to show our respect for others and ourselves?*
- *What can we do to help each person in the classroom community have self-respect and respect for others?*

LAYER 5: BOOK 4 (*ONE*)

Title: *One*

Author: Kathryn Otoshi

Illustrator: Kathryn Otoshi

2008 K O Kids Books ISBN 978–0972394642

"Blue is a quiet color. Red is a hot head. Red likes to pick on Blue. Yellow, Green, Purple, and Orange don't like what they see, but what can they do? When no one takes a stand, things get out of hand. Until One comes along and shows all the colors how to stand up and count." [from the publisher]

DAY 1: INTRODUCE THE BOOK

VISUAL TOUR/READING THE ART

As we view the art I'd like you to:

- notice the characters are just spots of color
- look for examples of how each color changes as we move through the pages
- notice how Red is larger, how his color is more opaque, how he gains size
- notice what happens to the other colors as Red gets bigger
- think about why this may be happening
- notice what happens when One shows up (Think about how this changes the dynamics of the situation.)
- notice how One's understandings and actions help others take action.

READ ALOUD

On the surface this is a very simple book. Read it through cover to cover and you'll discover there is great depth here. Read the book aloud with careful attention to pacing, tone, intensity, and mood. Move through this one slowly allowing your students time to take it in. In your initial reading to prepare for the read aloud, note those spots where tone shifts from bright to more somber or melancholy, where Red builds in intensity and power, where One stands firm. Let your voice reflect those emotions. Also note the shift in overall tone when Red is disarmed and begins to go away. Note the forgiveness and healing that comes from Blue. Let that shine through in your voice as well.

As I read I'd like you to listen for:

- how Blue feels and behaves most days
- how one bad thing can change everything else
- how the other colors are kind to Blue, but don't stand up for him (Think about why that could happen. What did they believe? Is there anything in the book to support what you are thinking? What have we learned from other books that help support your thinking?)
- how Red gets bigger and bigger (Why is that happening? How do the actions of the other colors effect this change?)
- the effect One has on all the colors. (Think about why that is.)

As I read I'd like you to think about:

- why One will stand up to Red and the other colors would not
- what changed inside the other colors that helped them decide to stand up for themselves and for others.

AFTER THE READ ALOUD

Close the book and sit with the language for a few seconds. Resist the urge to tell your students what they are supposed to understand. Sit in silence and expect them to do the same. After ten to fifteen seconds, speak in a quiet voice.

- **Think on your own:** *Let's pause here and think about the meaning of this book. What does this text suggest for you?* Allow about forty seconds for this. [Think/Write]

  If One had not come along and had not taken a stand, how would this situation be different? Think about the importance of one person. How can one person help bystanders gain the courage they need to help others?

  Think about Red. Why did Red pick on others? What happened at the end that may be a clue to understanding Red?

  Think about Blue. He was picked on. His friends liked him and said so, but they wouldn't help him when Red was being unkind. Think about why Blue was kind to Red at the end. Think about how Blue's kindness changed everything.

- **Stretch your thoughts with a partner:** *Now let's take about forty-five seconds to think together. Talk quietly with your partner, listen to your partner's ideas, share your thoughts, and think of a bumper sticker for this book.* [Share/Expand]

- **Share your new thinking:** *Let's share a few of your bumper stickers.* [Collaborate/Synthesize]

DAYS 2–3 EXTEND THIS THINKING UNTIL THE NEXT BOOK

Recall the insights from Layers 1 through 4. Revisit the bumper stickers from those books. In the next few days have students think and write about some of the following:

- *Think about the essential understandings we have charted as we studied each of the books so far. How do we see those understandings at work in this story?*

- *In this book Blue was picked on by Red. Then Blue was kind to Red and invited him to "count" along with all the other colors and One. Who is changed by this kindness? Is there a bumper sticker in this for our brains?*

- *What have we learned from One, the other colors, and Blue that we could do ourselves?*

- *Contrast the thoughts and beliefs of the other colors with those of One. How are the thoughts and beliefs of One like those of Molly Lou Melon and the dad in* A Chance to Shine?

- *Write your thoughts about how your new insights from our study can help change the attitude and behaviors of a bully.*

- *What can we do as a classroom community to make kindness matter?*

- *What can we do in our classroom to show our respect for others and ourselves?*

- *What can we do to help each person in the classroom community have self-respect and respect for others?*

LAYER 5: BOOK 5 (*THOSE SHOES*)

Title: *Those Shoes*

Author: Maribeth Boelts

Illustrator: Noah Z. Jones

2007 Candlewick ISBN 978–0–7636–2499–6

"All Jeremy wants is a pair of those shoes, the shoes everyone at school seems to be wearing. But his grandma tells him they don't have any room for 'want,' just 'need,' and what Jeremy needs are new boots for winter.... [A] young boy realizes that the

things he has—warm boots, a loving grandmother, and a good friend—are worth more than the things he wants." [from the publisher]

DAY 1: INTRODUCE THE BOOK

VISUAL TOUR/READING THE ART

As we view the art I'd like you to:

- notice the main character, Jeremy, seems to be longing for something (Look closely and see where his eyes are focused. Think about possible reasons he may want those shoes.)
- notice the other characters as we examine the art here (Think about what is beginning to happen here.)
- look at this illustration showing Jeremy's shoe coming apart (Think about what has happened to Jeremy's shoe. Notice the man on the right side of the page. Think about where Jeremy is and who that man is. Think about what is happening here and how Jeremy may be feeling.)
- think about which character could become a target of unkindness (What makes you think so?)
- think about which character or characters may use knowledge, understanding, and kindness to help another character
- notice the expressions and posture of most of the class when Jeremy comes back (Think about why this is happening.)
- notice the interactions between Jeremy and his grandmother in the next few illustrations (Think about what they are saying and thinking and feeling in these scenes.)
- take a close look at Jeremy's feet in the illustration showing Jeremy and his grandmother on the bed (Think about why his feet have all those bandages.)
- notice Jeremy's feet in the next several pages, and think about the shoes he is wearing (And notice his friend in the green hat and red scarf. Think about what Jeremy is considering here. What makes you think so?)
- think about Jeremy's act of kindness. (What does it tell us about the kind of character he is? How does it make Jeremy feel? How does it affect his friend Antonio?)

READ ALOUD

The main character, Jeremy, is the narrator in this book. He is a young boy who intensely desires a pair of the "in" shoes. This longing captivates his focus over most other things. As you read keep in mind that he longs to fit in, yet his family can't afford those shoes. Read the book aloud with careful attention to pacing, tone, intensity, and mood. There are moments where Jeremy has to face disappointment and he does so with grace and character even though he is feeling less than stellar about the situation. This is a longer read aloud than many others in the collection. Take your time; don't rush. The strength of Jeremy's character is revealed slowly. Your students will need the time to bring all their insights into play and to bring his character to the forefront of their conversations.

As I read I'd like you to:

- notice how important those shoes are to Jeremy (Listen for evidence in the text.)
- think about how Jeremy and Antonio are feeling
- think about why the shoes are so important to Jeremy
- think about why he doesn't have them
- notice what happens when Jeremy's shoe comes apart
- think about the kindness of Mr. Alfrey
- think about what Jeremy understands and what he worries about
- think about how the other kids behave when Jeremy comes in with his shoes from Mr. Alfrey's office (Think about why they are acting that way. What do they need to think about? What role are they playing in this story?)
- notice all the things Jeremy goes through to get a pair of those shoes (Think about how very important it is to him. Think about why he never wore them to school.)
- notice what Jeremy finally decides to do with his shoes. (Why does he do it?)

AFTER THE READ ALOUD

Close the book and sit with the language for a few seconds. Resist the urge to tell your students what they are supposed to understand. Sit in silence and expect them to do the same. After ten to fifteen seconds, speak in a quiet voice.

- **Think on your own:** *Let's pause here and think about the meaning of this book. What does this text suggest for you?* Allow about forty seconds for this. [Think/Write]

  Think for a moment about all the ways Jeremy and Antonio could be a target for bullies.

  Think about all the ways they are like every other human on the globe.

  Consider the act of kindness Jeremy displayed. What does that tell us about Jeremy and his grandmother? What do they understand?

  Think about Jeremy and Antonio. Do we see either of them change as the story unfolds? What's your evidence?

- **Stretch your thoughts with a partner:** *Now let's take about forty-five seconds to think together. Talk quietly with your partner, listen to your partner's ideas, share your thoughts, and think of a bumper sticker for this book.* [Share/Expand]

- **Share your new thinking:** *Let's share a few of your bumper stickers.* [Collaborate/Synthesize]

DAYS 2–3: EXTEND THIS THINKING UNTIL THE NEXT BOOK

Recall the insights from Layers 1 through 4. Revisit the bumper stickers from those books. In the next few days have students think and write about some of the following:

- *Think about the essential understandings we have charted as we studied each of the books so far. How do we see those understandings at work in this story?*

- *In this book Jeremy could have kept the shoes in his closet even though they were too small. Instead he gave them to his friend Antonio who needed new shoes. Does his kindness make a difference? Who is changed by this kindness? Is there a bumper sticker in this for our brains?*

- *What have we learned from Jeremy, his grandmother, Mr. Alfrey, and Antonio that we could do ourselves?*

- *What can we do as a classroom community to make kindness matter?*

- *What can we do in our classroom to show our respect for others and ourselves?*

- *What can we do to help each person in the classroom community have self-respect and respect for others?*

CHAPTER 7

Final Thoughts

Any one person can make a difference and everyone should try.

–John F. Kennedy

We enter these final pages knowing that each day children are stepping off buses, walking down the block, rolling in on their bicycles, hundreds of them arriving at school with backpacks bulging. Like a river they flow down the walkways into corridors and spill into classrooms just like yours, filling the space with a range of abilities and interests, an array of social-emotional issues. Each of them enters with the intense desire to belong and feel significant. As they step into the routine of the day, each of them longs to trust and be trusted, to value and be valued, to support and be supported.

We enter these final pages knowing that you are being asked to do more each year, the pressure to raise achievement levels increases while resources fail to keep pace. We know you are striving to meet all the needs of the children placed in your care. We know that you work diligently to ensure the physical and emotional safety of each child while the external demands hang in the air like thick smoke threatening to suffocate the joy of this work. We feel your frustration, share your determination, and stand with you in your dedication to doing what is best, what is right, what is necessary to ensure children leave school not only "well educated" but also as kind and civil beings who respect themselves and all of humanity.

We enter these final pages hoping we have provided you with an accessible and manageable resource. We've attempted to extend and deepen your professional knowledge about the culture of bullying in our schools. We designed the layered approach through the use of picture books to move in slowly, allowing students to contextualize the ideas and acquire the language for expressing their understandings. Moving slowly with time for reflection, conversation, and action is important for the development of empathy, confidence, and caring. We cannot rush, but we cannot wait.

It's a terrible thing to see and have no vision. —Helen Keller

While we wish there was no need for a book such as this in our schools, we know that bullying is and has been a well-established aspect of daily life for far too many students. We can see the problem. Now we have a vision, a plan of action, and each of us must work one classroom at a time to build strong, caring communities of learners. That begins when children learn to value themselves and others and begin to value their relationship with others. Working through these five layers, we strive to lead children to understand:

- I am one person, a member of the human family.
- I have much in common with all other people.
- All that makes me human is also present in all other people.
- Though there are differences among us, no difference makes one person more valuable than another.
- I gain nothing from being unkind to another person.
- I am responsible for my thoughts, my words, and my actions.
- I am responsible for the consequences of my choices.
- I make a choice to be kind or unkind.

In addition, through the read aloud experiences, reflections, conversations, and actions, we want to help students develop the skills needed to assess situations and evaluate their options. Children with a sense of self as one who is worthy, who respects the humanity of others, who recognizes the rights of all to dignity don't need the constant approval of others. Rather, they judge situations based on an inner strength and make choices that do not take dignity from others. Like Molly Lou, from *Stand Tall, Molly Lou Melon*, children learn from the examples of those around them, from significant, respected, and trusted others in their lives. In our classrooms, we can extend that learning to develop these skills and attitudes through rich conversations following read alouds that present social situations where characters are faced with choices and consequences.

If you could only sense how important you are to the lives of those you meet; how important you can be to the people you may never even dream of. There is something of yourself that you leave at every meeting with another person. — Fred Rogers

A Bit of Perspective

Each young person on the following list took his or her own life as the result of bullying. During their adolescence, a most fragile time in life, each one of these young people faced the impact of bullies, some of them for months or even years. For some it was physical and face-to-face. For others it was in the quiet and cowardly cyberworld. In either case another classmate (or group of classmates) gained a sense of power and a twisted pleasure through compromising the dignity of a fellow human being.

Notice these young people took their own lives between the ages of eleven and nineteen. They had lived. They knew life and found it unbearable to cohabitate with bullying. At some point each one of them could not escape, not in the comfort of family and home, not even in the private recess of his or her own mind. There was no place to escape the fear and anxiety of believing it will never end. Each of them left behind family and friends. Each of them was a student. Each of them spent his or her days in a school not unlike the places we work. Take a moment to turn on your computer, search each name below, and read the stories of these young lives extinguished by the suffocating presence of bullying.

Phoebe Prince, fifteen, Massachusetts

Carl Joseph Walker-Hoover, eleven, Massachusetts

Justin Aaberg, thirteen, Minnesota

Billy Lucas, fifteen, Indiana

Cody J. Barker, seventeen, Wisconsin

Asher Brown, thirteen, Texas

Harrison Chase Brown, fifteen, Colorado

Eric Mohat, seventeen, Ohio

Felix Sacco, seventeen, Massachusetts

Caleb Nolt, fourteen, Indiana

Jared B. High, thirteen, Washington

Ryan Patrick Halligan, thirteen, Vermont

Seth Walsh, thirteen, California

Tyler Clementi, nineteen, Rutgers University, New Jersey

Jamarcus Bell, fourteen, Indiana

Tyler Long, fourteen, Georgia

Jamey Rodemeyer, fourteen, New York

In one month alone (September 2010), nine teenage boys took their lives as a result of bullying. Suicide, the third leading cause of death in young people, results in 4,400 deaths each year. Research suggests a strong relationship between being the victim of bullying and suicide. In fact, it has been reported that victims of bullying are two to nine times more likely to consider suicide than nonvictims. And LGBT teens are four times more likely to be bullied.

According to the National Center for Educational Statistics, 28 percent of students from age twelve to eighteen reported that they were bullied in school during the 2008–2009 school year. Although bullying slows down as children get older (from a high of 39 percent of all sixth graders to 20 percent of high school seniors), it is still an oppressive presence in the lives of too many young people. The most overwhelming form of bullying is done through ridicule, insult, and rumors, rather than physical aggression. And it has been reported that 160,000 students per day miss school from fear of being bullied.

The ideas in this curriculum are intended to spark and lead a cultural change inside classrooms and schools. The work of that change is slow and deliberate. By design it is developed layer upon layer, working consistently like the force of water flowing over eons to create the Grand Canyon. A shift in consciousness is not typically something that occurs rapidly, so we must be patient and diligent. The books for this curriculum were selected to provide access to the essential understandings for each layer. Each layer scaffolds for the understandings in the next layer, to create an accumulation of understanding, not unlike the formation of a hailstone.

We fear the list will be longer by the time this book makes it to press. We cannot wait for a child from your school or district to be added to this list. We cannot wait for the cry for help. We cannot wait for a report from peers. We cannot wait. Martin Luther King, Jr. once said, "Now is always the right time to do the right thing."

Now. Yes, now!

We are already losing our children.

And Remember . . .

Bullying exists in almost every place people gather. The behavior emerges when any one of us fails to see ourselves, and all others, as fully worthy and fully human. No group, no region, no type of school is exempt. We have a chance to stop the bullying now. Together we can help students develop the insights and understandings essential to embracing their own humanity, respecting the humanity of others, standing together to resist bullying behavior, and coming to the defense of students being bullied. We close with these reminders:

1. A well-defined, safe learning community is essential to the development of healthy relationships among students. Community building builds a sense of belonging, a sense of power and place within the group, a sense of caring and responsibility for oneself and others, and an abiding respect for the members of the community.

2. Schools need to establish a policy regarding bullying. Students, educators, school staff members, and families must be made aware of the school and/or district policies regarding bullying behavior. The definition of bullying must be concise, widely communicated, and easily understood. All the players must understand the responsibilities of all parties as well as the consequences of bullying behavior.

3. Raising a moral child who embodies and can express empathy, self-control, self-respect, and respect for others is the responsibility of all adults in the life of a child.

Helen Keller has said, "Alone we can do so little; together we can do much." Let us embrace her wisdom and work together to prevent bullying in the lives of our children.

APPENDIX A

Additional Texts to Support Working Through the Layers

*Featured with a guided lesson in one of the layers and so is listed here without a summary.

*Whoever You Are**
*Skin Again**
*We Share One World**
*All the Colors of the Earth**
*Same, Same but Different**

Mirror [an excellent book to extend the thinking from *Whoever You Are* with older students]
Developed and Art by Jeannie Baker
2010 Candlewick Press ISBN 978-0-7636-4848-0

Open the book to find two books, each a mirror of the other. The book on the left illustrates the life of a boy living with his family in Australia. The book on the right illustrates the life of another boy living with his family in Morocco. Turn the pages in unison to see the "mirror" of life in two cultures, offering accessible opportunity to compare and contrast. You and your students will notice the differences in the details of daily life while recognizing those things that are the same for all people no matter where they live.

The Skin You Live In
Written by Michael Tyler
Illustrated by David Lee Csicsko
2005 Chicago Children's Museum ISBN 978-0-9759580-0-1

This delightful description of various shades of skin opens with a fun to read pattern and appealing illustrations. There is a clever twist as the author begins to talk about the many ways some people choose to think about differences: "It's not tall skin or short skin, or best in the sport skin: or fat skin or thin skin, you lose and I win skin." The ending is too good not to be shared: "And like flowers in the fields that make wonderful views, when we stand side-by-side in our wonderful hues . . . We all make a beauty, so wonderful true. We are special and different and just the same, too!"

We All Sing with the Same Voice
Written by Philip Miller and Sheppard Greene
Illustrated by Paul Meisel
2001 HarperCollins ISBN 0-06-027475-1

[From the jacket] "This joyful Sesame Street song embraces the notion that no matter where children live, what they look like, or what they do, they're all the same where it counts — at heart!" The book describes many children showing differences in hair and eye color. It points out how children live in different countries and feel a full range of emotions. Yet all of them like to do many of the same things: run and climb, sit and read, watch TV, and go to sleep. The art is joyful and will have children hanging on your every word. A CD is included.

Two Eggs, Please
Written by Sarah Weeks
Illustrated by Betsy Lewin
2003 Aladdin ISBN 978-0-689-83198-6

What happens when we focus only on the differences on the outside of things rather than looking at the inside as well? This book perfectly illustrates the idea. From the outside eggs do look different but when cracked open the insides are the same. Sarah witnessed a kindergarten teacher inviting her students to do this activity and she came away with an idea. The book features various animals in a café ordering eggs in many different ways: sunny side up, over easy, scrambled, soft boiled, hard boiled, etc. Each time an order is made one of the animals recognized that they are all different . . . but the same.

Fill a Bucket (Lower)
Written by Carol McCloud and Katherine Martin
Illustrated by David Messing
2008 Ferne Press ISBN 978-1-933916-57-6

Growing Up with a Bucket Full of Happiness: Three Rules for a Happier Life (Upper)
Written by Carol McCloud
Illustrated by Penny Weber
2010 Ferne Press ISBN 978-1-933916-57-6

This is a perfect upper grade companion for McCloud's *Fill a Bucket*, which is written for younger children. The focus is making good choices and supporting one another. Each book conveys the message that our words and actions are choices we make and that we are responsible for our choices. Both books are written in clear and simple language.

LAYER 2: Moving In: There Are Ways In Which We Are Different— Not Less Than Others, Not Better Than Others, Just Different

Ian's Walk *
Mama Zooms *
Moses Goes to a Concert *
The Pirate of Kindergarten *
The Colors of Us *

Different Just Like Me
Written and Illustrated by Lori Mitchell
1999 Talewinds Books/Charlesbridge ISBN 1-57091-490-7

On a trip with her mom, April realizes though children around her are different in many ways they are just like her in many others. While on the bus and walking down the street, April notices how children look different from each other. She notices one girl uses her hands to talk yet she waves hello the same way April does. Later April notices children come in all different sizes and shapes but each of them smiles just the same. And on the elevator April notices a lady who finds her way with the help of a guide dog and reads words written in Braille with her fingertips to find the right floor. April discovers just how much she has in common with everyone around her.

Can You Hear a Rainbow? The Story of a Deaf Boy Named Chris
Written by Jamee Riggio Heelan
Illustrated by Nicola Simmonds
2003 Peachtree ISBN 1-56145-268-8

One book from a series inviting us to explore the world through the perspective of children with special needs. Each book in the series offers an important opportunity to gain insight into another's point of view. This book and each of the other titles in the series can be a springboard into deepening our understanding of how there is no difference that sets any one of us outside the common bonds of humanity.

The Hickory Chair
Written by Lisa Rowe Fraustino
Illustrated by Benny Andrews
2001 Arthur A. Levine/Scholastic ISBN 0-590-52248-5

Louis and Gran have a special bond. He was born blind and she reads to him in the chair Gramps carved from an old hickory tree that once grew on the property. When Gran dies, she leaves all her grandchildren something that will remind them of her and their love for one another. But Louis doesn't find the note she left for him until one day as he sat in her hickory chair, his finger finds the hole in the cushion, a memory from his childhood. Inside that hole he finds a note and with the note, Gran left him the hickory chair.

Bright Eyes, Brown Skin
Written by Cheryl Willis Hudson and Bernette G. Ford
Illustrated by George Ford
1990 Just Us Books ISBN 0-940975-23-8

In this very short text four young children go to school brimming with confidence about all the ways they are alike. You can guide your children to discover all the ways they are different: shade of skin, clothing, shape of face, color of hair, etc. This can open the conversation about how differences do not make us better than others or less than others. *Bright Eyes, Brown Skin* is an easy text for young children to discuss alike and different.

LAYER 3: Inside the Circle: Thinking, Feeling, Acting

*Be Good to Eddie Lee**
*Bee-Wigged**
*Hooway for Wodney Wat**
*Odd Velvet**
*Camp K-9**

The Orange Shoes
Written by Trinka Hakes Noble
Illustrated by Doris Ettlinger
2007 Sleeping Bear Press ISBN 978-1-58536-277-6

Delly lives with her family on a farm outside of town. They walk to school each morning along a dirt road. Because Delly's family is poor, they mostly go barefoot, which is fine with Delly until she gets to school and has to sit beside Prudy Winfield, who has many pairs of shoes and taunts Delly because she is barefoot. When Miss Violet makes an announcement about a Harvest Festival, Delly longs for a pair of shoes to wear. However, her Dad needs all the money he has saved for tires for the truck. To her surprise he buys only two tires so that he can buy her the pair of shoes she wants so badly. She can't resist taking them to school the next day only to have Prudy ground her foot right down on Delly's toe. Several others join in and the shoes are scuffed and scratched and one button even got lost. All seems lost until Delly paints tiny flowers on the shoes to cover all the scratches. One reading and you will celebrate what happens at the festival. Who will sell their lunch box for the most? Rich Prudy or poor Delly?

Each Kindness
Written by Jacqueline Woodson
Illustrated by E. B. Lewis
2012 Penguin ISBN 978-0-399-24652-4

When a new girl (Maya) comes to town wearing hand-me-down clothes Chloe doesn't want to be her friend and turns away from her at every opportunity. Maya repeatedly offers tokens of friendship, but at every turn she is rebuked. As the days pass Maya stays to herself more and more until one day her desk is empty and the class finds out that she will not be returning to school. Their teacher brings a large bucket of water into the classroom and demonstrates how a pebble dropped into the still water causes ripples reaching the very edge. She equates the dropping of a pebble with an act of kindness. Chloe's classmates begin to name kind things they've done for others, but when it is Chloe's turn she freezes and thinks of all the times she turned her back on Maya. As the story closes Chloe says to herself, "I watched the water ripple as the sun set through the maples and the chance of a kindness with Maya becoming more and more forever gone."

The Cow That Went Oink
Written and Illustrated by Bernard Most
2002 Voyager Books (Harcourt) ISBN 978-0-15-220195-1

All the animals in the barnyard have quite a time making fun of a cow that oinks and a pig that moos. Both the cow and pig become very sad being the object of such ridicule. Through their tears they become determined to make the sounds they are expected to make. They work hard to change and finally succeed in learning to make the expected sounds. But they have the last laugh, being the only animals that could make more than one sound.

Lizette's Green Sock
Written and Illustrated by Catharina Valckx
2002 Clarion ISBN 0-618-45298-2

Lizette finds a lovely green sock. She falls in love immediately and thinks of her find as a treasure until the neighborhood boys tease her saying how useless one sock is. She looks and looks for the mate to the green sock. The boys find the mate but throw it away into a lake so they could continue to tease Lizette. Fortunately, Lizette's friend Bert sees the possibilities of the one green sock and he wears it like a cap. During all the searching Lizette's mother knits another green sock so the friends have matching caps. And as a little twist, a tiny fish adopts the tossed green sock as a bed. So the teasing boys don't win after all.

Say Something
Written by Peggy Moss
Illustrated by Lea Lyon
2004 Tilbury House ISBN 0-88448-261-8

African Proverb: "If you think you are too small to make a difference, try sleeping in a room with a mosquito." The story tells about several children who were picked on but no one intervened. Although the narrator doesn't enter in on the bullying, she doesn't step into the situation to just "say something" either. One day all her friends were out so she sat alone at lunch. This set her up for ridicule by a group of boys. That taught her the pain of being the one singled out, so the next day she chose to befriend one of the kids who had been bullied. By doing so she found a new friend and learned an important lesson.

Ella
Written and Illustrated by Carmela and Steven D'Amico
2004 Scholastic ISBN 978-0-439-62782-4

[From inside flap] "The littlest elephant in Little Village is also just a little bit shy. She's moved to a new neighborhood, and has to start at a brand-new school. Good thing she has her grandma's lucky hat to take along. But Belinda Blue, the bully, doesn't like Ella. And she doesn't like the hat. And that means trouble with a capital 'B.'" Your children will fall in love with Ella as she stumbles through her first days with a sad heart when all her classmates join Belinda is teasing and making fun of her. Read with delight how little Ella wins over all as she conquers her fears to save Belinda.

The Bully from the Black Lagoon
Written by Mike Thaler
Illustrated by Jared Lee
2004 Scholastic ISBN 978-0-545-06521-4

Sometimes the thought of a bully is far worse than the bully. Fears grow with each thought and rumors spread like a virus infecting everyone. This is the case for a new kid named Butch Pounders. Rumor had it this guy was one big bad bully, as big as Coach Kong, transferred from the state pen, and the rumors get bigger and bigger as the fear and dread become unbearable. Yet, when Butch shows up he is nothing like the fears that preceded him. Perceptions and rumors, oh my!

LAYER 4: At the Core: When Others Are Not Thoughtful, Caring, and Kind

Bootsie Barker Bites*
Dog Eared*
The Recess Queen*
The Bully Blockers Club*
Bully*

Bailey the Big Bully
Written and Illustrated by Lizi Boyd
1989 Viking ISBN 0-670-82719-3

A very short text with a powerful message: It's more fun having friends than being bullies. Bailey was a bully who demanded his way regardless of what he and his classmates were doing. He was bossy and made up his own rules. But when Max moved to town, things begin to change. Max simply stood up to Bailey and soon everyone was ignoring Bailey and going to Max's house to play. One day Max invited Bailey over and he tried to bring his old ways with him. This time everyone stood up to him and pretty soon Bailey nailed a sign up at the base of the tree house that said "Bullies Keep Out!"

Nobody Knew What to Do: A Story About Bullying
Written by Becky Ray McCain
Illustrated by Todd Leonardo
2001 Albert Whitman ISBN 0-8075-5711-0

"Nobody likes to think about it, even though we know it is not okay to hurt a person with words, or things, or with the way we behave." As with most schools, there is a bully and no one knows what to do about him. Everyone is afraid to intervene until one day a classmate can stand it no longer and goes to the rescue of Ray, the victim. "Together we know what to do and say to make sure bullying is NEVER okay. We work together to make it end." An author's note can be found in the back giving you suggestions about bully prevention.

Bully
Written and Illustrated by Patricia Polacco
2012 Penguin ISBN 978-0-399-25704-9

At her new school Lyla discovers that she and Jamie like many of the same things. They become fast friends. However, when Lyla makes the cheerleading squad, she becomes more popular with the "in" group and soon forgets all about her friend Jamie. She begins to dress differently and spends all her extra time with Gage and the cool kids. But when the group begins to tease and make fun of others using Facebook, Lyla begins to question her choices. When she moves away from the group they turn on her in an even more vicious way. The ultimate insult happens the week of the state test when the principal discovers a test is missing. Because Lyla makes the best grade in the school they immediately accuse her. Lyla's innocence is not revealed until Jamie comes forward to admit that he saw Gage slip into the room and take a copy of the test. Lyla's dad helps her understand the bullying behaviors of others when he explains, "in order for people like Gage's candle to glow brighter, she has to blow out yours."

Lucy and the Bully
Written and Illustrated by Claire Alexander
2008 Albert Whitman ISBN 978-0-8075-4786-1

Lucy loves school but as in many classrooms there is a bully who breaks her things. At first the teacher excuses Tommy because she doesn't want to think he is being a bully on purpose. His behavior continues, which sends Lucy home each day sad and discouraged. She tries to work it out on her own because she doesn't want to tell her mother. But her mother finds out and calls the teacher once Lucy goes to bed. Now Tommy doesn't want to go to school either. However, Lucy's heart is in the right place and at art time she compliments Tommy's work. No one had ever done that before and Tommy was surprised. He apologizes to Lucy for making fun of her and tearing up her things. Before the day is over, they are playing together at recess.

Hats
Written and Illustrated by Kevin Luthardt
2004 Albert Whitman ISBN 978-0-8075-3171-6

This almost wordless picture book is elegant in its simplicity. With very minimal text and vivid illustrations, Luthardt conveys a powerful message. A young boy comes upon a hat sale and selects his favorite before even going into the store. He is delighted with his choice until he meets the neighborhood bully waiting for him in the park. The bully makes fun of his hat and suddenly he is unsure of his choice. He feels dejected until first one friend and then another comes along and compliments his new hat. The three friends head to the park with a soccer ball. When the bully makes fun of all three hats, the boy demonstrates strength and kindness by inviting the bully to play and then complimenting the bully's hat. The tone changes and now there are four friends.

Shrinking Violet
Written by Cari Best
Illustrated by Giselle Potter
2001 Melanie Kroupa/Farrar, Straus and Giroux ISBN 978-0-374-36882-1

Violet is a talented girl but hates for anyone to pay attention to her. She is especially shy when she gets in front of her classmates, and Irwin makes her want to shrink because he teases her so much. When the teacher announces a school play and that everyone will take a part, Violet panics. Violet knew the parts by heart and when Irwin messes up the night of the play Violet steps in and steals the show leaving Irwin to "fidget and burp and twiddle his thumbs." The audience loved the play and Irwin even told Violet he was sorry he had said such mean things to her.

Loudmouth George and the Sixth-Grade Bully
Written and Illustrated by Nancy Carlson
1983, 2003 Carolrhoda Books ISBN 978-1-57505-549-7

George, a kindergartner, encounters Big Mike, the sixth-grade bully who demands his lunch each morning as George is walking to school. By week's end, George is a nervous wreck and his friend Harriet decides how to take care of Big Mike. Over the weekend, they prepare a "delicious" lunch, which when eaten breaks Big Mike from picking on little kids and demanding their lunch. And Harriet gains a little backup from her cousin Lance, just in case.

Stay Away from RAT BOY!
Written by Laurie Lears
Illustrated by Red Hansen
2009 Albert Whitman ISBN 978-0-9075-6789-0

Tyler bullies everyone. He pushes and snatches and makes fun of everyone in his class. He doesn't seem to want a friend, but he does like the class pet, a rat named Snowball. So Tyler becomes known as the Rat Boy. When Snowball escapes, Tyler is very upset and searches everywhere for him. Jose, a classmate, begins to feel sorry for Tyler and misses Snowball as well so he sets out to help. When the boys find the pet, Jose tells Tyler his dad will build a bigger cage so Snowball will be happier in the classroom. Because of their love for the pet, Tyler sees the goodness in Jose and they become friends.

Henry and the Bully
Written and Illustrated by Nancy Carlson
2010 Penguin ISBN 978-0-670-01148-3

Henry and his first-grade friends love playing soccer during recess. But one day Henry runs into the back of Sam (Samantha), a new second grader, as he is chasing the ball. Sam kicks their ball over the fence and the other second graders laugh. By the weekend Henry claims to be sick and begs his mom not to make him go to school. When he realizes it is Saturday his stomachache suddenly goes away. On a shopping trip with his mom, he sees Sam trying on a dress that she hates. Sam really turns up the heat for fear Henry will tell all the people at school but instead on Monday Henry invites Sam to play soccer with his friends.

Chester Raccoon and the Big Bad Bully
Written by Audrey Penn
Illustrated by Barbara Gibson
2008 Scholastic ISBN 978-0-545-20395-1

Shortly after beginning school, Chester and his friends beg to stay home from school. Wise Mrs. Raccoon suspects something is bothering them and begins questioning and supporting them in loving ways. She offers to walk them to school and help them solve the problem with the bully. She doesn't dismiss any of their fears and gives them security by walking with them. She tells them sometimes bullies don't know any other way to be. Through a story she advises them how to stick together and to work as a group to stand up to the bully badger.

The Three Bully Goats
Leslie Kimmelman
Illustrated by Will Terry
2011 Albert Whitman ISBN 978-0-8075-7900-8

In this version of a beloved fairy tale the three *bully* goats are known for their bullying ways so no one dared disturb them. They weren't satisfied in their meadow and felt the other side of the river offered better grazing. The problem was that many small animals called that meadow home and the ogre that lived under the bridge was protective of them. The ogre knew he would have to be very clever to convince the goats that the meadow was not for them. He teased them by reminding them that the tallest grass was usually the best and tastiest grass of all. What he didn't tell them was that the tallest grass was home to a family of skunks! Well before long those bully goats rushed back to their own meadow where they didn't have to deal with skunks, and the grassy meadow was returned to the small creatures.

The Ant and the Big Bad Bully Goat
Written by Andrew Fusek Peters
Illustrated by Anna Wadham
2007 Child's Play ISBN 978-184643-079-4

Badger kept his home neat and tidy where everything had a place. One day when he went to the garden to pick vegetables for his dinner, Bully Goat rammed in and locked the door. Badger came back and politely asked to be let in but Bully Goat told him no way, it was his house now. Badger went all around the farm asking for help from all the animals but everyone was too busy. In the meantime Bully Goat was tearing up Badger's house. He drank up all the milk, ate up all the honey, and left everything broken. When Ant saw how heartbroken Badger was, he offered to help rid him of the Bully Goat. When Bully Goat saw the little screaming Ant he laughed and knew he could smash the Ant with no problem. However, when the Ant stung Bully Goat's nose he fled crying and never returned. Badger and Ant became the best of friends for the rest of their lives.

You're Mean, Lily Jean!
Written by Frieda Wishinsky
Illustrated by Kady MacDonald Denton
2009 Albert Whitman 978-0-8075-9476-6

Carly and Sandy are sisters and best friends. Every day they play together—dragons and knights, mountain climbers and astronauts. But one day Lily Jean moves in next door and immediately changes the dynamics of playtime. She demands to have Sandy's attention and begins bossing Carly around, giving her the role of baby or royal dog. Though she is very hurt, she takes the demands until one day she can stand it no more. Her solution is creative.

Freckleface Strawberry and the Dodgeball Bully
Written by Julianne Moore
Illustrated by LeUyen Pham
2009 Bloomsbury ISBN 1-59990-316-4

Freckleface Strawberry loves to go to Early Bird school when her parents must go to work early. On the playground she gets to play all sorts of fun games. She dreads rainy days when they must play dodgeball inside because Windy Pants Patrick is such a bully. He throws balls at all the kids too fast and too hard. It always hurts but he won't stop. One day she learns to stand in back of all the other kids and use her imagination to dream up a monster who can stand up to Windy Pants. Lost in her imagination she doesn't realize all the other kids are out and she is standing alone. What will she do to survive the next hard throw? How will she deal with Windy Pants? When he throws, Freckleface realizes the ball didn't hurt because she used her imagination to become the monster that roars back and suddenly Windy Pants is the one who is scared.

LAYER 5: Getting Focused for Action: An Opportunity to Explore the Actions of Others, Reflect on Our Own Feelings, and Redirect Our Behaviors Toward Fellow Human Beings

*Stand Tall, Molly Lou Melon**
*Hey Little Ant**
*A Chance to Shine**
*One**
*Those Shoes**

Feathers and Fools
Written by Mem Fox
Illustrated by Nicholas Wilton
1989, 2000 Voyager Books ISBN 0-15-202365-8

When we focus on difference and fail to see our common bonds, it is easy to become distrustful and to view others as less than worthy. In the allegory Mem Fox aptly reminds us how a focus on difference can lead to fear and result in destruction. In the story a pride of peacocks and a flock of swans live side by side until each of them begins to notice, then fear, their differences. This thought-provoking book can be used with any age group beyond third grade. It has the potential to spark deep discussion and raise awareness of the power of our perceptions of others.

Fabulous! A Portrait of Andy Warhol
Written and Illustrated by Bonnie Christensen
2011 Christy Ottaviano ISBN 978-0-8050-8753-6

As a child Andy suffered from St. Vitus' dance, an illness that caused muscle spasms and permanently blotchy skin, making him the target of taunts. Christensen takes us into the world of Andy Warhol and reveals how he worked to overcome the unkind treatment of others. Though Andy retreated into his sketches as a way to escape throughout his childhood, it was not until he was a young man that his genius began to shine, overshadowing those differences. *Fabulous* is a lesson in perseverance.

Oliver Button Is a Sissy
Written and Illustrated by Tomie dePaola
1979 Harcourt Brace Jovanovich ISBN 0-15-257852-8

Oliver doesn't like to play baseball or football like the other boys. He would rather draw and read instead. But above all he likes to dance. Other kids tease him and call him a sissy. His parents are confused because their son is different but when he asks to take dance classes they allow him to enroll. Oliver enters the school talent show and though he doesn't win the competition he does become a top-rated dancer. Soon his family and classmates stop their ridicule of his "sissy" ways.

The Juice Box Bully
Written by Bob Sornson and Maria Dismondy
Illustrated by Kim Shaw
2011 Ferne Press ISBN 978-193391672-9

This one provides an opportunity to explore the power of community where each person makes a pledge to care for the others. The text presents various episodes of bullying and opens the door to conversations about the choices we make and what it means to stay true to your word. The book ends with a pledge, called the Promise:

> I WILL speak up instead of acting as a bystander.
> I CHOOSE to participate in activities that don't involve teasing.
> I FORGIVE others if they make poor choices.
> I MODEL good behavior.
> I ACCEPT others for their differences.

I INCLUDE others in group situations.

I AM powerful in making a difference in my school.

How to Lose All Your Friends
Written and Illustrated by Nancy Carlson
1994 Puffin ISBN 0-14-055862-4

This is a clever book for young children packed with advice about how to lose all your friends:

1. Never smile.
2. Never share.
3. Be a bully.
4. Be a poor sport.
5. Tattle.
6. Whine!

Each page of advice is followed by an explanation of what doing each of these things will do to the people around you. For example, bullies pick on little kids, push in front of the lunch line, and play mean tricks on kids. And, of course, the true message shines through . . . this is no way to live.

Snail Started It
Written by Katja Reider
Illustrated by Angela Von Roehl
1997 North-South books ISBN 0-7358-1142-3

Snail carelessly says to Pig, "You so fat I am surprised those legs hold you up." Though not affected at first, Pig later feels the sting of the hurtful words. He in turn says hurtful words to Rabbit who in turn says hurtful words to Dog and on it goes until the hurtful words come back around to Snail. When words hurt him he realizes he must apologize and goes in search of Pig. Pig then realizes his mistake and goes in search for Rabbit. Thus the cycle of forgiveness begins.

Emily Breaks Free
Written by Linda Talley
Illustrated by Andra Chase
2000 Marsh ISBN 978-1-55942-155-3

Emily loves going for her morning walks but on this day she breaks free and runs from her mistress to chase down her Frisbee. The problem she soon encounters is Spike, the bully of the neighborhood. He grabs Emily's Frisbee and off he goes. Spike suddenly invites Emily to stroll along with him. Flattered by the invitation, Emily quickly forgets all about her mistress. On their stroll they meet up with Cotton, a small fluffy dog tied up outside a shop, and Spike snatches the little dog's treat. Emily shares the biscuit but it doesn't taste as good as she expected because she can't escape the hurt on Cotton's small face. Now Emily is not feeling so good about being with Spike and regrets her decision. As Emily is trying to decide how to make things right a kind and wise dog, Emerson, shows her the way.

Martha Walks the Dog
Written and Illustrated by Susan Meddaugh
1998 Sandpiper ISBN 978-0-395-90494-7

Words can make a difference. Bob was the bully of the neighborhood because his owner was also a bully who yelled at Bob and kept him chained up under the front porch. Bob made every animal in the neighborhood miserable with his menacing bark. Martha decides to teach Polly the parrot to say positive things rather than "bad dog," which were the only words anyone ever said to Bob. One day after Bob breaks loose from his chains he chases Martha, who runs for her life. Just as she gives up and prepares to die the words from Polly save her: "Good dog! Good dog!" Bob smiles and his tail begins to wag.

One of Us
Written by Peggy Moss
Illustrated by Penny Weber
2010 Tilbury House ISBN 978-0-88448-322-9

Roberta moves to a new school and each group in the school wants her to join them. She moves from the group of girls who wear their hair up, to those who like to play on the monkey bars, to the group with flowers on their lunch boxes, to the group who all have pitas for lunch. The problem she found was that if you fit in with one group, you couldn't be friends with someone in another group. Finally she gets fed up and decides to just sit alone because she likes what she likes. In the end you find her with a group who enjoy just being who they are and don't care for the "all or none" attitude of the other groups.

Ferdinand
Written by Munro Leaf
Illustrated by Robert Lawson
1936 Puffin ISBN 0-14-050-234-3

Ferdinand was completely happy being himself. But his differences made his mother worry. She wanted him to run and butt heads like all the other little bulls. As the years passed, Ferdinand grew into a big strong bull that still loved sitting under his tree enjoying solitude. When the bullfighters came to recruit new bulls for the bullfights, they overlooked Ferdinand until suddenly a bee stung him and he reared up snorting, looking very fierce. Poor Ferdinand was taken away in their cart. On the day of the fight they stuck him with pins but all Ferdinand did was go to the center of the ring, sit down, and smell the lovely flowers in the hair of all the ladies. The matador finally realized Ferdinand wasn't going to fight, so they took him back home where he moved immediately to his favorite tree and sat quietly smelling the flowers.

A Bad Case of Stripes
Written and Illustrated by David Shannon
1998 Scholastic ISBN 978-0-439-59838-5

Even though Camilla loved lima beans, she wouldn't eat them because none of her friends would and she wanted to be just like them. She wanted to dress like them, but on the very first day of school as she was fretting over what to wear she looked in the mirror and discovered she was completely covered in bright stripes. She was mortified! The doctor could find nothing wrong with her so she was sent to school. However, she continued to change stripes according to what activity she was doing. She was causing quite a disturbance at school with the kids laughing so she was sent home. Suddenly she was so famous that the TV crews came to her house to see for themselves. They tried everything to rid her of the stripes, but nothing worked until an old woman showed up and found the "real" Camilla hiding inside of herself who wouldn't eat lima beans even though she wanted them. From that day on Camilla ate lima beans every time she wanted them and she never developed a case of stripes again.

Hands Are Not for Hitting
Written by Martine Agassi, Ph.D.
Illustrated by Marieka Heinlen
2009 Free Spirit Press ISBN 978-1-57542-308-1

An excellent book to open a conversation with young children about being friends in a learning community rather than bullies who demand to have things their way. The book begins: "Hands come in all shapes, sizes, and colors. There are lots of things your hands are meant to do." Several pages later the contrast is given: "There's something that hands are NOT for. Hands are not for hitting. Hitting isn't friendly." The text is simple with a powerful message.

Words Are Not for Hurting
Written by Elizabeth Verdick
Illustrated by Marieka Heinlen
2004 Free Spirit Press ISBN 1-57542-156-9

This very short and simple text will open conversation with young children about how words can be used for good things but also for very hurtful things. The text helps explain that your words belong to you and you are responsible for choosing the words you use. Discuss how it feels when someone says words to you such as: "You can't play with us. You're stupid! Your clothes are ugly!" Then contrast those hurtful words with words such as: "Let's work together. Do you want to share this with me? I'm glad we're friends." This short one can become a wonderful foundational book for building community.

Not My Fault
Written by Leif Kristiansson
Illustrated by Dick Stenberg
2006 Heryin ISBN 978-80976205661

When you are a witness to someone being bullied, you have choices and those choices have consequences. In this understated text, the role of bystanders is in the spotlight and it becomes clear that believing "it's not my fault" isn't enough. To be present but do nothing, or to participate in some way while absolving yourself because you didn't start it, is a choice. There is a shift in the final pages, moving from one specific situation to more global ones, and we are faced with the question: Does it have nothing to do with me? This small book illustrated with simple line drawings and six poignant black-and-white photographs poses deep questions worthy of reflection and much conversation.

Talk Peace
Written by Sam Williams
Illustrated by Mique Moriuchi
2005 Holiday House ISBN 0-8234-1936-3

This simple text with limited print and vibrant art reminds us that we have the opportunity to talk peace, to live peace, in all that we do. In that process the art makes subtle contrasts that could be the springboard for more in-depth conversation.

Somewhere Today: A Book of Peace
Written by Shelley Moore Thomas
Photographs by Eric Futran
1998 Albert Whitman ISBN 0-8075-7545-3

A simple presentation pairing one sentence with a full-page photo reminds us that at this moment somewhere on this globe someone is making a choice to perform an act of kindness. The message is simple but clear: each one of us is responsible for the choices we make. Each one of us can choose peace or strife, kindness or unkindness.

CHAPTER BOOKS

Bullies Are a Pain in the Brain
Written and Illustrated by Trevor Romain
1997 Free Spirit ISBN 978-1-57542-023-3

An entertaining, humorous text with cartoonlike illustrations conveys an important message. *Webster's Dictionary* defines a bully as "a blustering, browbeating person; especially one who is habitually cruel to others." In other words, bullies are people with problems. They like to hurt and frighten people they see as smaller or weaker. Experts tell us that bullies like to be in control. By controlling you, a bully feels strong and superior. And you feel puny, afraid, and angry. Though deceptively simple in format, this book offers substantial advice. While older students will manage this independently, you could share it with younger students as a read aloud along with conversation.

My Big Mouth
Written by Peter Hannan
2011 Scholastic ISBN 978-0-545-16210-4

Moving to a new school is difficult whether you're in first grade or ninth grade and moving in the middle of the year makes it even harder. For Davis, the move is difficult so he decides that blending in will be the best way for him to escape attention. He really doesn't care if he has friends or not. But when Davis starts a band, he becomes the center of the attention of the entire school including the school bully, Gerald "the Butcher" Boggs. At one point Davis tries to befriend the Butcher, but when he addresses him as "Gerald," all he gets is a black eye. You won't put the book down until you find out who ends up with whom and which boy gets which girl. Hannan sprinkles engaging sketches throughout the book.

In or Out
Written by Claudia Gabel
2007 Scholastic ISBN 978-0-439-91853-4

What happens to a lifelong friendship when you get to high school? What happens when one friend starts outgrowing the other? Nola and Marnie are about to find out that life changes when you move to a bigger arena where new people put new pressure on you. Lizette and her little trio of friends run the school with threats and dares adding to the tension. The book is well written and many teenage girls will identify with the cast of characters.

Losers
Written by Matthue Roth
2008 Scholastic ISBN 978-0-545-06893-2

Here's one for high school students that will equate bullying with being a loser. The back of the jacket offers a checklist to know whether you are a loser. Do you:

- listen to music that's not popular
- hang out with math geeks
- read poetry
- come from another country
- get embarrassed easily in overly social situations
- worry that everyone else is hooking up more than you?

If you answer yes to any of these questions, there are people who think you're a loser but not Jupiter Glazer, the social outcast of the school. He is sexually insecure. He wants to stay apart from others but decides if he continues on this path he will lose out on enjoying his days in high school. These eleven chapters tell the story of his journey, highs and lows, through high school.

Amy Hodgepodge: All Mixed Up
Written by Kim Wayans and Kevin Knotts
2008 Penguin ISBN 978-0-448-44854-1

Amy has been homeschooled for years and is excited to enter fourth grade in a "real" school. Her first day is met with teasing not only because she has been homeschooled and she is new, but also because she looks different. Amy is part Asian, Caucasian, and African-American. She finds new friends and one affectionately gives her a nickname (Amy Hodgepodge) since she has mixed heritage. With her new friends Amy discovers many ways they are all the same.

We Want You to Know: Kids Talk About Bullying
Written by Deborah Ellis
2010 Coteau Books ISBN 978-1-55050-417-0

This collection of interviews with students between the ages of nine and nineteen provides insight into the thoughts and feelings of bullies, bystanders, and victims. Each vignette is followed by an opportunity to pause, reflect, and talk in response to a few questions posed under the heading, "What do you think?"

Bullying and Me: Schoolyard Stories
Written by Ouisie Shapiro
Photographs by Steven Vote
2010 Albert Whitman ISBN 978-0-8075-0921-0

Each page features one of thirteen young people sharing the story of his or her experience with bullying. Each vignette is paired with color photography and advice from Dr. Dorothy Espelage, a noted expert on adolescent bullying. The book concludes with tips on dealing with bullies.

Bystander
Written by James Preller
2009 Square Fish (Macmillan) ISBN 978-0-312-54796-7

Preller introduces a thirteen-year-old boy who moves to a new school to begin seventh grade. The most popular boy in the class, Griffin, wants to be his friend. Before long Eric is uncomfortable with how Griffin treats others. Yet it takes Eric some time to figure out how he can stand up to Griffin without becoming his victim. School officials know about the problem but don't make an attempt to intervene, so Eric's decisions become even more important. An interview with Preller is included.

Safe at Home
Written by Sharon Robinson (daughter of Jackie Robinson)
Cover Illustration by Kadir Nelson (son of Sharon Robinson)
2006 Scholastic ISBN 0-439-67197-3

Following the death of his dad, Elijah J Breeze, known as Jumper, and his mom are forced to move back to Harlem to live with his grandmother. Jumper likes nothing about the city. He had spent his whole life in Connecticut where he enjoyed lots of friends, swimming, playing basketball, and soccer. While his mother is wrapped up in her grief, Jumper feels lost and resentful. Left to his own devices, Jumper soon runs into the neighborhood bully. After his mother enrolls him in the local baseball club (much to his grief), he finds the bully is one of the better players. The coach is a very wise man who works miracles in the lives of his players, showing them what getting along and supporting others really means.

Playground
Written by 50 Cent with Laura Moser
Illustrated by Lizzi Akans
Penguin 2012 ISBN 978-1-59514-434-8

This book is packed with issues that will undoubtedly spark conversations that will linger long after the final chapter is read. The story revolves around a young boy who gets the nickname "Butterball" soon after his mom moves them from New York City out to the suburbs. They move so the mom can attend nursing school, leaving fun-loving dad behind. All of this fills Butterball with anger and resentment. At his new school everyone ignores him except for one small boy named Maurice. When Butterball finally gets up the nerve to invite Maurice over for a visit, Maurice suggests something Butterball has never even considered—his mom and her new girlfriend may be partners rather than friends. At that point Maurice becomes enemy number one and Butterball is determined to make Maurice pay for his comments. Now everything in Butterball's world goes wrong and with each bad decision things go from bad to worse. The book will hold your interest from the first line to the final page when Butterball begins to turn his life around to become a wise young man who seeks to correct all his mistakes.

APPENDIX B

Sample Parent/Guardian/Caregiver Letter

Dear Parent/Guardian,

We are committed to creating a bully-free learning community in our school and our classroom this year. One important aspect of a learning community is a healthy respect for self and others paired with an attitude of acceptance for all others in the school.

The goal is for every person in our community to work toward having a win-win attitude in working out any conflict that may occur at school. I invite you to be an active part of developing this community by asking your child each day to discuss the events that happen at school. I need your support and your participation if the win-win attitude is to become a habit of being in daily life. Encourage your child to demonstrate the same attitudes and practices at home.

It is important to realize that for children to grow academically, they must feel safe and have a strong sense of belonging. Therefore, if a situation occurs at school and has not been resolved, it is very important that you make an appointment to inform me of the facts surrounding the event. Bullying will not be tolerated and will be addressed if it ever occurs.

All members of our class will be involved in activities throughout the year to help them develop the language needed to explain their thoughts, feelings, and actions when comments or behaviors cause them to feel uncomfortable, insignificant, or unheard. Our guidelines will include kindness to everyone, respect for all, compassion for others, and an effort to always strive for peace.

Thank you for your support! You can reach me at _____ if you have questions, concerns, or suggestions.

Sincerely,

Estimado padre/tutor,

Estamos comprometidos para tener una área "sin abusos (intimidación) entre estudiantes" en nuestra comunidad de aprendizaje en este año escolar. Nuestros objetivos son de proporcionar a su hijo una clase basada con respeto y la aceptación por cada miembro de nuestra clase. La meta es que cada persona en nuestra comunidad, pueda lograr ser un ganador en la elaboración de cualquier conflicto que se produce en la escuela. Le invitamos a unirse en esta jornada preguntando a su hijo todos los días sobre los acontecimientos que suceden en la escuela. Para que sea un ganador debe unirse a nosotros en este esfuerzo.

El centro de nuestros esfuerzos se iniciará mediante la lectura de libros que ayudan a establecer las situaciones que se abren conversaciones acerca de cómo tratar y entender el comportamiento de un compañero que abusa de otros. Leeré lecturas y tendremos actividades en el cual hablaremos del tema sobre el abuso de los compañeros y su comportamiento. Además hablaremos que podemos hacer si estamos en una situación como esta.

Es importante darse cuenta de que los niños al crecer académicamente, deben sentirse seguros y tener un fuerte sentido de pertenencia a la comunidad escolar. Por lo tanto, si su hijo tiene un problema en la escuela que no ha sido resuelto, es imprescindible que usted haga una cita para informarme de los hechos que hayan ocurrido. El abuso, intimidación no serán tolerados y debe ser abordado si alguna vez ocurre.

Cada miembro de nuestra clase estarán involucrados durante todo el año al centrarse en este problema social que es muy importante y que afecta no sólo a nuestro salón de clases, pero a las vidas de nuestros hijos también. Queremos que los niños tengan el lenguaje necesario para explicar las cosas que los hagan sentir incómodos e insignificantes. Nuestras guías académicas se incluye, la bondad, el respeto de todos, la compasión por los demás y un esfuerzo por luchar siempre por la paz.

Usted es muy importante para nuestro esfuerzo y le invitamos a que nos acompañen en este esfuerzo. Visítenos a menudo.

Gracias por su apoyo! Usted puede comunicarse conmigo al _____ si usted tiene preguntas o sugerencias.

Atentamente,

APPENDIX C

Sample Antibullying Pledge

We the students of _____ school agree to work together to stop bullying in our school.

Bullying is defined as intentionally aggressive behavior that can take many forms (verbal, physical, social/relational/emotional, or cyberbullying—or any combination of these), and involves an imbalance of power, and is often repeated over a period of time. Bullying can involve only one child bullying another, or a group of children ganging up against one lone child, or one group of kids targeting another group.

Common behaviors attributed to bullying include put-downs, name-calling, rumors, gossip, verbal threats, menacing, harassment, intimidation, social isolation or exclusion, and physical assaults.

We believe that no student deserves to be bullied. We believe that every student regardless of race, color, ethnicity, religion, country of origin, size, gender, sexual orientation, popularity, athletic ability, academic success, or social skill has the right to feel safe, secure, and respected.

Therefore I agree to:

- treat all other people with kindness and respect
- be a good role model for other students
- be aware of the school's antibullying policies and procedures
- abide by the school's antibullying policies and procedures
- support students who have been victimized by bullies
- speak out against bullying in any form including verbal, relational, and physical and cyber
- notify a parent, teacher, or school administrator if bullying does occur.

_____ Student's Signature

_____ Parent's Signature

_____ Date

Adapted from Carpenter and Ferguson (2009), *The Everything Parent's Guide to Dealing with Bullies*, p. 279.

APPENDIX D

Activities for Community Building

Ideas to Build Community

Learn the names of all your classmates.

This is an essential step toward getting to know our classmates. Knowing someone's name opens up communication. So, try this simple but effective routine. Sit in a circle. Hold a beanbag in your hand, look around the circle and say, "Good morning, my name is [state your name]." Make eye contact with another person, toss the beanbag to that person and ask, "What is your name?" Upon catching the beanbag, that student introduces herself, "Good morning, my name is [states her name]." She then makes eye contact with another student, tosses the beanbag to him, and the process continues. As the last student introduces himself the beanbag is tossed back to you.

Add handshakes (K–6) from Responsive Classroom (www.responsiveclassroom.org).

A few weeks into the school year, when students are more comfortable with each other and with the format of greetings, you might add the following variations to the basic good morning greeting: a handshake, a high five, a high five and an ankle shake, a pinky shake, a touch on the shoulder, or an elbow shake.

Add marbles greeting (K–6) from Responsive Classroom (www.responsiveclassroom.org).

This is a quick greeting. Each child has three marbles or other small objects. When the teacher says, "Go," students mingle, greeting each other by saying, "Good morning [state the name of the person]." Every third person that a student greets gets a marble. When all original marbles have been given away, the student sits down.

I know your name and something you like.

After a few mornings of learning the names of classmates, add a layer. Perhaps it will be a comment about favorites (music, author, color, food, place to visit). It would go something like this: "Good morning, my name is [state name] and my favorite music is [state preference]." You begin the circle to model the expectation, then toss the bean-bag to the person you are greeting. (Journal entry: Write about how it feels when people use your name and know something about you.)

Draw a self-portrait.

Provide each child in the room art paper with crayons and a mirror if possible. Ask children to draw their face. Make a ceremony out of placing these colored self-portraits on the wall of the classroom and leave them on the wall. Have your own self-portrait ready to show the children what you are asking them to do. Place your portrait on the wall before asking them to draw their faces. Have their names written on label-size tag board or simply print their names or have them write their names on their portraits. (Journal entry: Write about drawing your face, what you notice about yourself, and how it felt to see your face up on the classroom wall with the faces of all your classmates.)

Name your emotions.

Introduce the Feeling Chart (happy face, sad face, angry face, worried face, surprised face, etc.). Hold a small beanbag in your hand and say, "Good morning, my name is [state your name] and today I feel [state your emotion and show that expression on your face]." Then toss the beanbag to a student. He or she holds the beanbag and repeats the action you just modeled until all students have had an opportunity to say their name, name their attitude, and model one of the faces on the feeling chart. (Journal entry: Write about what happens to make you happy *or* write about the emotion you feel today and what has happened to make you feel that.)

Develop positive thoughts about yourself and others.

Gather the group in a circle, place a bucket in the center, and give each child a few objects (marbles, for example). Begin by modeling the expectation. "Good morning, my name is [state your name] and I can [state something that you feel successful with]." Then place one of your marbles in the bucket. Continue around the circle in turn having each child say his or her name and one thing he or she feels confident with before placing a marble into the bucket. *Note*: You can extend the activity by asking each child to repeat what the one before him has stated (for example, "Her name is [repeat name] and she is good at [repeat name of activity]. My name is [state name] and I'm good at [state activity]"). (Journal entry: Write about one thing you do well and how you feel when you do something well, *or* write about how you feel when others do well.)

Acknowledge our strengths and the strengths of others.

After a few weeks of school, write each child's name (and yours) on a slip of folded paper and place the names in the bucket in the center of the circle. Begin the cycle to model the expectation. Go to the bucket, draw out a slip of paper, and return to your place in the circle. Unfold the slip and insert the name in this statement: "[State the name on the slip] is helpful because he [state something positive about having that person as a member of the community]." (Journal entry: Write about using your talent/strength to help someone in need. Set a goal for the week, *or* write about how all the different strengths in your classroom make a better community. Set a goal for the community.)

Find the heart of the matter.

Give each child a sheet of paper with a large heart printed in the center. Ask each student to write his or her name at the top of the heart and to fill the inside with things that matter most to him or her. These may be family, friends, pets, places, events, objects, memories, etc. Bring students back to the circle to share with each other. Post these in the room and invite children to explore their common passions. As with any other activity, complete your own heart to use as an example. Follow up with a community heart, perhaps on a bulletin board, where you list the common passions of the group. (Journal entry: Write about what you discover you have in common with others. Think about what it means to be with others who share your interests. Also think about what it means to know people who have interests that are different from yours.)

Take responsibility to help make the world a better place.

Using a sheet of colored paper (cover) and two sheets of white paper folded in half and stapled, have ready one booklet for each student. In the meeting circle read aloud *Miss Rumphius* (Cooney 1985) (or another title where the main character's focus is making the world a better place). Following the reading, initiate a conversation about Miss Rumphius and the attitudes, beliefs, and actions that define her character. Summarize these characteristics on a chart for the students to see. Invite all the students to think of something they could do to make the world a better place. Ask them to share their thinking with the person next to them. Invite a few children to share something they are planning to do or something a classmate told them. Then, share your own thought and model how you make an action statement out of that (e.g., "I think the world would be a better place if people tried to help their neighbors. So, this is my promise. This week I am going to offer to rake the leaves in my neighbor's front yard because she is not able to do it herself"). Continue around the circle, inviting each student to each tell his or her plans for doing something good for his or her world. When all children have shared, ask them to write their pledge and draw themselves doing it on the cover. Place these in a special labeled basket for others to read.

Extend the experience with role-playing and decision making.

Tell the students you are going to role-play an action you've witnessed and you'd like them to think of reactions that would help change the situation. Model for them both roles.

First scenario: "You can't play with us if you're going to play with her!" Ask partners to discuss why someone would say something like that. Then invite a few students to tell how they will react if they hear someone saying this.

Second scenario: "I'm having a party Saturday but you aren't invited!" Ask partners to discuss this social situation and what they would say and feel. Invite a few children to tell how they will react if they hear someone saying this to another student. Then invite a few children to tell how they will react if someone says this to them.

Third scenario: "Let's run over and help Mrs. Smith pick up her apples." Ask students to think about why someone would want to help a neighbor when they could be playing. Invite partners to discuss, then invite a few to share.

Fourth scenario: "Our classroom always gets messy by the end of the day. Let's begin working together to make it shine before we go home." Ask students to think about why someone would want to work when they could just wait and let another person clean up the mess. Ask partners to discuss then invite someone to share.

Discuss wounding words.

Gather the students in a circle. Read aloud *Snail Started It!* (Reider and von Roehl 1999) or *Mr. Peabody's Apples* (Madonna 2003). Each of these stories provides a demonstration of how words can hurt. Before the story is read, bring the bucket full of marbles to the center of the circle. Explain that the bucket filled with marbles represents a person. Read the story. Then tell the children we are going to take marbles out of the bucket each time someone does something that is unkind. When Snail says something unkind to Pig, invite a child to remove a marble from the bucket. When Pig says something unkind to Rabbit, invite another child to remove a marble. When Rabbit insults Dog, invite a third child to remove a marble, and so on. When the plot reverses and apologies are offered, return one marble with each apology. Remind children that once words are said, you can't take them back but an apology does help. (Journal entry: Draw a line dividing the page in half. On the left side of the page list ways we can remove marbles from someone's bucket and on the right side list ways we can put marbles into someone's bucket.)

Use a popular song with movements created by Responsive Classroom (www.responsiveclassroom.org).

Form an inner and outer circle facing each other. Partners are facing each other and the chant begins:

> Hello, neighbor, what d'ya say? (Wave to partner.)
>
> It's gonna be a wonderful day. (Circle arms to form an arc over your head, then lower your arms to your sides.)
>
> Clap your hands and boogie on down. (Clap hands to the beat while you wiggle down and back up.)
>
> Give me a bump and turn around. (Gently bump hips and turn all the way around and return to the position facing your partner.)

At the end of the chant, the students in the inner circle move one student to the right and the chant begins over again. This can continue until each inner child has greeted all the students in the outer circle if you want it to last that long.

Suggestions Adapted from Caring School Community (www.devstu.org)

Welcome new students (K–1).

Invite the class to gather in the meeting area. Remind the students that in a community we work hard to be responsible for ourselves and to treat each other with respect, kindness, and caring. We help one another and try to make everyone feel safe and welcome. Tell them that a new student is coming and you need them to think about ways to make the new student feel welcome.

Ask if anyone has ever been the new student in class. If so, ask those students to talk about what that first day was like for them.

Ask them to think about what might be difficult about being a new student coming into the class. Invite your students to talk with their partner and share ideas. Then have a few children share with the group what they learned from their partners.

Invite the group to help you generate a list of ways the class can help the new student feel welcome. You may begin the discussion by asking, "What are some things a new student would need to know if she came into the classroom today?" Record their responses on a chart. You may also ask the group to help you think of some jobs or activities they can do as a class to help the new student feel welcome. Add these responses to the chart.

Get ready for a substitute teacher (K–1).

Invite the class to gather in the meeting area. Remind the students that we are working on building community in our classroom. Explain that today we are going to discuss how to be responsible and helpful when you are absent and the class has a substitute teacher. Explain the role of the substitute ("A substitute will be your teacher when I can't be here. Whenever I have to be absent I will always talk to the substitute or leave notes about our class so he or she will know what to do.").

Ask the students to think of ways each of them can make the substitute feel welcome to our community at the beginning of the day. Allow time for them to think, turn and talk with a partner, and share the ideas they have come up with. Record the suggestions on a chart.

To tighten the responses, you may want to be specific with your questions:

What can you do to help the substitute's day go more smoothly?

What are the most important things you need to remember to do during the day?

What can you do to help the substitute when it is time for lunch?

What can you do to show you are responsible when it is time to go out to recess (go home, etc.)?

Draw closure to the activity by writing a letter to the substitute using many of the suggestions made by the children. For example:

Dear Substitute Teacher:

Welcome to _____,

Here are some ways we will be responsible and helpful while you are here.

At the beginning of the day, we will help you learn our names. When it's time for lunch, we will show you how we use our lunch cards and clean up. When it's time to go to recess, we will put our things away in our cubbies and line up quietly.

Thank you for being our teacher today.

Sincerely,

Ideas for Role Playing

(Adapted from *Bully Free Zone in a Jar*. Published by Free Spirit Publishing.)
Situations to open up conversation in the classroom:

- Three children walking home from school when one kid bullies another kid with one kid acting as the bystander.
- One kid is being threatened by another to give up their snack money.

- Four kids at a ballgame and two begin to gossip about a kid from school. What do the other two kids do?

- Your best friend asked you to let him or her copy your homework because they forgot to do it. What do you do?

- Three kids on the playground and one gets mad and kicks his or her classmate. When the teacher's attention turns to the problem, what will the third kid say when both kids are friends and he or she doesn't want either to be in trouble?

- You get a nasty email about a kid at school who has been mean to you. You know the email is untrue. How do you react?

- You report a bullying incident to your teacher but the teacher doesn't do anything about it. What do you do?

- The bully in your classroom who has made your life miserable all year apologizes to you during lunch. What do you do? How do you react?

- You and your best friend are at the mall when someone bumps into you, making you spill your drink. How do you react?

- Your friend's big brother smashes your bike and your friend gets mad at you because you get upset. How do you handle the situation?

APPENDIX E

Resources for Educators

Starting Small: Teaching Tolerance in Preschool and the Early Grades, by the Teaching Tolerance Project. 2008. Southern Poverty Law Center.

The International Bullying Prevention Association: www.stopbullyingworld.org.

The following items are all taken from ABC News:

"The Bully Project" Outreach Campaign and Film: a documentary examining bullying in America over the span of one year. The associated website, www.thebullyproject .com, offers suggestions for assistance if you are the victim of a bully or if you witness bullying of another individual. You can also find information on the Facebook page at www.facebook.com/TheBullyProject.

U.S. Department of Health and Human Services' "Stop Bullying Now" Campaign: www.stopbullying.gov is an official U.S. Government website managed by the Department of Health and Human Services in partnership with the Department of Education and Department of Justice. There are specific tabs for kids, teens, young adults, parents, educators, and the community. Each tab contains information targeted to the age group with information in cartoon format for the youngest and brief video clips for older students. The information is accessible, concise, and focused. There is also information specific to LGBT bullying/violence and cyberbullying.

National Crime Prevention Council on Cyber-Bullying: This website, www.ncpc.org /cyberbullying/, provides clear information targeted to teens regarding what cyberbullying is, how to recognize it, how it occurs, what you can do to prevent cyberbullying and remain cybersafe. This page is a section of the website for the National Crime Prevention Council site. Most children and youth will recognize the character "McGruff," the crime dog mascot for the organization.

Gay, Lesbian, and Straight Education Network (GLSEN): A national organization de-voted to assuring that each member of every school community is valued and re-spected regardless of sexual orientation or gender identity/expression. Among many efforts, GLSEN works with educators, policy makers, community leaders, and students to protect students from bullying and harassment. You can find more information on the website at www.glsen.org.

The Trevor Project: A national organization providing crisis intervention and suicide prevention services to lesbian, gay, bisexual, transgender, and youth questioning their sexual orientation or gender identity. The website www.thetrevorproject.org hosts a blog, news updates, tweets, and a nationwide 24–7 crisis intervention lifeline.

Office on Women's Health, www.girlshealth.gov/parents/parentsbullying/index.cfm, provides information for parents, educators, and caregivers on recognizing the signs of bullying and talking with their daughters/female students about bullying behav-iors. All the information is available in Spanish with one click. Several other websites listed as additional resources.

PBS Kids, "It's My Life" Page: The most kid-friendly page we've found. The website, www.pbskids.org/itsmylife, is very easy to navigate and has several sections with in-formation kids will find pertinent. There are sections focused on bullying with clear, concise language discussing what it means to be a bully, types of bullying behavior, and what to do if you are either a witness or a victim.

BIBLIOGRAPHY

American Psychological Association. APA bullying page, accessed April 12, 2012, www.apa.org/topics/bullying/index.aspx.

Beane, A. 2005. *Bully Free Classroom.* Minneapolis, MN: Free Spirit Publishing.

———. 2009. *Bullying Prevention for Schools: A Step-by-Step Guide to Implementing a Successful Anti-Bullying Program.* San Francisco, CA: Jossey-Bass.

Brunn, P. 2011. "Quick Thoughts on Bullying in School." Developmental Studies Center blog, October 5, 2011, www.devstu.org/blogs/quick-thoughts-on-bullying-in-school.

Carpenter, D., and C. Ferguson, 2009. *The Everything Parent's Guide to Dealing with Bullies.* Avon, MA: Adams Media.

Chaney, R. S. 1991, 2002. *Teaching Children to Care: Classroom Management for Ethical and Academic Growth, K–8.* Turners Falls, NY: Northeast Foundation for Children.

Coloroso, B. 2011. "Bully, Bullied, Bystander . . . and Beyond." *Teaching Tolerance* 39: 50–53.

Coloroso, B. 2009. *The Bully, the Bullied, and the Bystander.* New York: HarperCollins.

Common Core State Standards. 2011. www.corestandards.org.

Cooney, Barbara. 1985. *Miss Rumphius.* London: Puffin.

Developmental Studies Center. 2009. *Caring School Community Leadership Guide.* Oakland, CA: Developmental Studies Center.

Dosani, S. 2008. *Bullying: Brilliant Ideas for Keeping Your Child Safe and Happy.* Oxford, United Kingdom: Infinite Ideas.

Drew, N. 2010. *No Kidding About Bullying.* Minneapolis, MN: Free Spirit Publishing.

Free Spirit Publishing. 2010. *Bully Free Zone in a Jar: Tips for Dealing with Bullying.* Minneapolis, MN: Free Spirit Publishing.

Kaufman, G., L. Raphael, and P. Espeland. 1990, 1999. *Stick Up For Yourself.* Minneapolis, MN: Free Spirit Publishing.

Madonna. 2003. *Mr. Peabody's Apples.* New York: Callaway.

Main, M., and D. Weston. 1981. "The Quality of the Toddler's Relationship to Mother and Father: Related to Conflict Behavior and the Readiness to Establish New Relationships." *Child Development* 52: 932–40.

Olweus, D. 1993. *Bullying at School: What We Know and What We Can Do.* Carlton, Victoria, Australia: Blackwell.

Olweus Bullying Prevention Program. 2011. Available at: www.olweus.org/public /bullying.page.

PBS Kids. 2009. It's My Life. Available at: http://pbskids.org/itsmylife/.

Peterson, R. 1992. *Life in a Crowded Place: Making a Learning Community.* Portsmouth, NH: Heinemann.

Reider, K., and A. von Roehl. 1999. *Snail Started It!* New York: NorthSouth Books.

Responsive Classroom. 2007, 2008. *Responsive Classroom Level I Resource Book.* Turner Falls, MA: Northeast Foundation for Children.

Sroufe, L. A. 1988. "The Role of Infant-Caregiver Attachment to Development." In *Clinical Implications of Attachment,* edited by J. Belsky and T. Nezworski. Mahwah, NJ: Lawrence Erlbaum Associates.

Staton, D., R. Hogan, and M. Ainsworth. 1971. "Infant Obedience and Maternal Behavior: The Origins of Socialization Reconsidered." *Child Development* 43: 1057–69.

Swearer, S. M., D. L. Espelage, and S. A. Napolitano. 2009. *Bullying Prevention and Intervention: Realistic Strategies for Schools.* New York, NY: Guilford Press.

Voors, W. 2000. *Bullying: Changing the Course of Your Child's Life.* Center City, MN: Hazelden.